THE COMPLETE
CROCK POT COOKBOOK
FOR BEGINNERS

3000 Days of Easy, Delicious, and Effortless Slow Cooker Recipes for Every Meal, from Breakfast to Dinner, Snacks, and Desserts

LYDIA HARCOURT

Table of Contents

INTRODUCTION

You've just returned after an exhausting workday. You're hungry, you're tired, and the prospect of cooking something from scratch seems daunting. When you open the refrigerator and look through the contents, nothing seems to be screaming "dinner." Your stomach rumbles, the clock is ticking down, and the temptation to order takeout is strong. Do you recognize this? For many of us, it seems unachievable to balance the responsibilities of everyday life with the desire to cook healthful meals. But what if I told you there was a method to make a meal that tastes like it took hours of work out of the odd things you have in your kitchen, without actually having to spend those hours?

This is where your trusty slow cooker, or crock pot, steps into the role of culinary hero. In a world where time seems to be slipping away from us, the crock pot comes to the rescue, making it easy to prepare filling, tasty meals. Imagine this: you throw a few basic ingredients into the pot in the morning, set the timer, and your house smells like a gourmet creation by the time you get home in the evening. Your family and friends will be amazed by the recipes in this book and believe you've slaved away all day over the stove when, in fact, the crock pot worked its culinary magic.

This book came about as a result of a profound comprehension of the challenges faced by busy individuals in the kitchen. I had experienced the struggle myself after years of juggling a work and providing meals for my family. Cooking is usually the last thing you want to do on a stressful weeknight. However, microwave dinners and fast food don't exactly satisfy. Something that is both nourishing and convenient is what you need. I've put together this list of slow-cooked meals in order to help you get back some of your time without compromising on taste or nutrition.

Probably the reason you're here is since you're sick of looking at ingredients and not knowing what to do with them. It's possible that you've attempted a few crock pot recipes in the past but found them to be boring or uninspired. Alternatively, perhaps you've never used a slow cooker before and are unsure of where to begin. I understand. There are many cookbooks that give the same old options—stews, soups, and more stews—but not all crock pot recipes are made equal. However, this book is not like the others.

You'll find a range of recipes in these pages, from tasty dinners to delightful desserts, all created to maximize the capabilities of your slow cooker. You'll discover how to make delectable chocolate lava cake, creamy curries, soft ribs, and melt-in-your-mouth pot roasts using common, everyday ingredients. The finest aspect? These recipes won't need you to watch over them. When it's ready, just set it, forget about it, and enjoy.

Here's what you can expect as you dive into this cookbook:

- **Time-Saving Techniques:** Toss everything into the crock pot before you go for work and come home to a cooked supper, learn how to prepare meals ahead of time.

- **Budget-Friendly Meals:** You can create wonderful, soft dishes with inexpensive items like seasonal vegetables and harder pieces of meat by slow cooking them.

- **Healthy Options:** You'll find many of healthy, balanced, and flavorful slow-cooked dishes here, dispelling the myth that these dinners are heavy.

- **Versatile Recipes:** This cookbook has recipes for every occasion, whether you're cooking for a large group of people or preparing meals for the next week.

- **Minimal Effort, Maximum Flavor:** Impressive dishes don't require you to be a trained cook. I'll demonstrate how to use a small number of components to bring forth complex flavors.

Not only am I providing recipes, but also a solution to the nightly "what's for dinner?" question. You won't dread meals with this book. Instead, you'll look forward to finding what's been cooking all day, knowing the work will be worth it.

Over the years, I've tried several ways to simplify cooking without sacrificing taste. I've taught busy parents, professionals, and inexperienced cooks how to use crock pots as culinary tools. My method is to use fresh, readily available ingredients, a little ingenuity, and a crock pot. To ensure each recipe tastes great, I've spent years experimenting with combinations, cooking times, and flavors.

I know, are these recipes really that easy? Yes, they can. Slow cooking lets flavors develop and ingredients break down better than rapid cooking. Slow and low is crucial. Imagine fork-tender meats or veggies that have absorbed the rich, savory juices from hours of simmering. That's crock pot magic.

But this cookbook goes beyond convenience. Reviving kitchen bliss. It's about making meals you'll be proud to serve, whether for a family dinner or a special event. Even when time is short, I want you to feel confident in the kitchen and create something great. The cooking matches your life, not vice versa.

The recipes in this book provide recommendations for adapting them to your tastes. Unlike a spice? Swap it. Like your veggies firmer? Adjust cooking time. These recipes are versatile so you can customize them. I encourage you to try different flavors and enjoy slow cooking.

In today's hectic environment, we often have to pick between quick meals and hours in the kitchen. The crock cooker eliminates the need to pick. Both are possible. This cookbook shows you how to make slow-cooked dishes that taste like you spent all day cooking but just took minutes. This book will be your go-to for easy, delicious dinners for beginners and pros alike.

If you want to simplify dinner and experience slow cooking, this book is for you. Start making amazing dishes with minimal ingredients in a crock pot—dinner doesn't have to be complicated.

CHAPTER 1:
A Slow Cooking Revolution

The Birth of the Crockpot

The simple yet revolutionary Crockpot has changed how families cook since its invention. The Rival Company introduced the Crockpot in the 1970s to make cooking healthy meals easier without continual supervision. Its capacity to turn cheap ingredients into gourmet dishes with little effort made it appealing to working families, busy professionals, and anyone who didn't have time to cook.

Slow cooking methods were used by home cooks before the Crockpot. Slowly cooking meals on the stove or in the oven for hours was customary. These methods required near-constant care and risked overcooking or scorching food. With its self-regulating, low-heat cooking approach, the Crockpot provided constant, hands-off cooking. This breakthrough revolutionized the culinary landscape and food preparation in countless homes, not just a tool.

The Science Behind Slow Cooking

A slow cooker maintains a constant low temperature for extended periods of time. Tenderizing and flavoring tough slices of meat is achieved by slowly releasing heat, which breaks down the connective fibers. Cooking at higher temperatures can remove moisture from food, whereas cooking it at lower degrees preserves its moisture.

The removable ceramic or stoneware pot is held in place by a heating source inside the crockpot. A heating element encircling the saucepan distributes the heat uniformly. All the way from 170°F (77°C) to 280°F (138°C), the gadget maintains a consistent low temperature as a result of construction. Cooking in this manner prevents food from scorching or boiling.

One major benefit of cooking slowly is the way the flavors blend. In contrast to rapid cooking, slow cooking allows the tastes of the various ingredients to meld, resulting in a dish with more depth and richness. Cooking stews, soups, and roasts slowly brings out their inherent flavors and improves their flavor.

A Time-Saving Solution for Modern Life

The Crockpot, a kitchen time-saver, gained popularity in the second part of the twentieth century, as people's lives became busier. When it acquired popularity, society was in the process of transforming itself. When more women entered the workforce, families sought ways to balance employment, household responsibilities, and cooking. The Crockpot's portability made it suited for these new ways of life. Slow cooking's "set it and forget it" feature enables customers to start their meals in the morning, go for a run, and return home to a ready-to-eat supper.

It made home-cooked meals more accessible to busy people by making cooking easier and decreasing the demand for takeaway and pre-packaged foods. The trend toward quick and easy meals that don't sacrifice nutrition or taste reflected a larger social change.

The Rise of One-Pot Meals

In today's kitchens, one-pot cooking has been transformed by the Crockpot. One-pot meals are preferred by practical cooks since they require fewer dishes and save time. You may prepare a whole meal in one pot with minimal preparation.

Add the vegetables, proteins, and liquids to a Crockpot recipe, then set it to cook. Unlike sautéing or roasting in separate pans, which need numerous steps, this method is different. Balanced meals are the outcome of letting food release its flavors gradually and harmoniously through slow cooking.

There's no shortage of one-pot recipes. Classics cooked in a slow cooker include pulled pork, chili, and soups made with chicken or vegetables. These hearty, flavorful recipes require very little cooking. Slow cooking allows meats to become soft, veggies to soak liquids, and flavors to develop.

Healthy Cooking: An Unanticipated Benefit

The key selling feature of the Crockpot upon its introduction was convenience. The health advantages of slow cooking became apparent as its usage increased among individuals. Slow cooking retains vegetable and protein constituents more effectively than high-heat frying, promoting a healthier diet.

Utilizing a Crockpot for cooking reduces fat content, which constitutes one of its primary benefits. Utilizing a Crockpot allows for the preparation of various oil-fried or sautéed dishes while significantly reducing calorie and cholesterol intake, as it eliminates the need for added fats. The natural oils in meats are released during slow cooking, eliminating the necessity for supplementary fats to improve flavor and texture.

The technique of slow cooking at low temperatures is also effective for diminishing salt levels. Slow cooking enhances flavors, necessitating less salt than baked or stovetop foods. The Crockpot is ideal for individuals avoiding salt and adhering to low-sodium diets.

Meal Planning and Budget Cooking

Budget meal planning is simplified by crockpot cooking. Numerous households are apprehensive about food prices. Its efficacy lies on transforming inexpensive cuts of meat into exquisite meals using a Crockpot. Beef chuck, pork shoulder, and chicken thighs become soft and flavorful after prolonged slow boiling.

Energy efficiency constitutes an additional advantage of the Crockpot. The Crockpot consumes less electricity than an oven for several hours. The minimal energy use renders long-term meal preparation more economical.

Batch cooking in the Crockpot streamlines meal preparation and conserves energy and materials. A substantial amount of chili or stew prepared on Sunday can be utilized throughout the week. Bulk cooks and meal planners utilize frozen and reheated remnants.

Expanding Culinary Horizons: International Flavors in the Crockpot

The Crockpot is adaptable enough to cook a wide variety of cuisines, despite its American origins. Its extensive simmering and braising times make it appropriate for ethnic dishes that require long cooking times to develop deep flavors. Other recipes that work well in a crockpot include tagines, braised meats, and curries.

In Indian cuisine, the slow cooker may cook chicken tikka masala, butter chicken, and lentil-based dals. Slow simmering infuses spices into meat or veggies, creating deep, complex tastes typical of Indian cooking. Mexican slow-cooked carnitas, barbacoa, and mole sauce may be made easily in a Crockpot.

Traditional Moroccan tagines, cooked in a clay pot at low heat, work wonderfully in a Crockpot. Slow simmering enhances the dish's sweet and savoury characteristics, especially when using dried fruits, almonds, and preserved lemons. Adventuresome home cooks eager to try global flavors without expensive equipment or expert cooking techniques use the Crockpot.

Crockpot Cooking in a Sustainable Kitchen

The Crockpot is a product that aligns with the philosophy of sustainability, which is prized by contemporary cooks. The Crockpot reduces the environmental impact of food preparation by requiring less energy than an oven or cooktop. Its mass cooking reduces food wastage by allowing for the freezing or consumption of large quantities over a period of few days.

Furthermore, the Crockpot promotes the consumption of whole foods, thereby reducing the necessity for processed foods. Rather than purchasing pre-cooked meals or processed treats, home chefs can use the Crockpot to prepare nutritious meals from scratch using fresh, unprocessed ingredients. The growing movement to restrict the consumption of industrial foods, which are detrimental to human health and the environment, is consistent with the emphasis on whole foods.

The capacity to prepare meals with in-season vegetables and less expensive meat promotes sustainable cookery. Slow cookers reduce the environmental impact of food production by utilizing the entire animal or locally grown produce.

The Modern Crockpot: Technology Meets Tradition

Modern technology has enhanced the functionality of the Crockpot, but there have been few modifications since the 1970s. Programmable schedules, a variety of heat settings, and smartphone connectivity for remote control are all features of contemporary slow cookers.

The Crockpot is now more user-friendly for tech-savvy home chefs who require precise control, thanks to these updates. Users may establish a timer to cook in the morning and instruct the machine to transition to "keep warm" mode upon completion. Individuals with unpredictable schedules will benefit from this feature.

The versatility of the kitchen is enhanced by the ability of certain varieties to sauté, steam, or pressure cook in a single pot. These advancements demonstrate that slow cooking has evolved to accommodate the requirements of contemporary families.

The Crockpot's Cultural Impact

A crockpot is a sign of the balance between old and new values, as well as the ease of making home-cooked meals. It has changed how people cook, eat, and spend time together because so many people use it.

An aroma of a Crockpot food that has been cooking for a long time can bring comfort and memories back to many people. It's linked to family meals, getting together, and not having to worry about anything. Families get together, potlucks, and other community events are incomplete without crockpots, which can cook a lot of food instantly.

Online communities and social media have brought the crockpot back to life. Websites, blogs, and social media all have slow cooker recipes, tips, and ideas that you can use. As fans share their recipes, a new group of home cooks learns how easy and versatile slow cooking can be.

The Crockpot Revolution

The Crockpot is a valuable appliance in contemporary kitchens due to its user-friendliness, health benefits, and versatility. This instrument has evolved from its rudimentary origins to a vital kitchen component, transforming culinary practices by integrating traditional and contemporary methods.

In a hectic environment, its deliberate and systematic cooking process provides a moment of tranquility and comfort. The Crockpot enables individuals to prepare delectable home-cooked meals with minimal effort. This has rendered it a widely utilized instrument in households around.

CHAPTER 2:
The Science of Slow Cooking

The slow cooker, also called a crockpot, is an important appliance for every home because it can turn simple items into delicious meals without any help. The crockpot's draw lies in its ability to cook food slowly for long periods of time, softening tough cuts of meat and mixing different ingredients to make flavors that go well together. To understand how slow cooking works, we need to look at how the crockpot is made, how heat moves, how chemicals change, and other unique features. The scientific concepts behind slow cooking are explained in this chapter, along with the parts of a crockpot and the chemistry involved in using one.

The Anatomy of a Crockpot

Before we can figure out how a crockpot works, we need to look at what makes it up. Even though crockpots come in a few different sizes and shapes, they are all built with similar parts that work together to cook food slowly and evenly.

1. **The Outer Casing:** The outside of the crockpot is made of metal or plastic. Around the inside of the pot, it holds the burning element in place. The outer shell keeps the heating device safe and sends heat to the food inside.

2. **The Heating Element:** In the exterior shell is the heating element, usually metal coils or ceramic resistive heaters. This generates heat for cooking. This element distributes heat evenly throughout the pot's bottom and sides, keeping food from burning like with direct heat.

3. **The Inner Pot (Crock):** A replaceable, hefty ceramic or porcelain inner pot rests inside the outer case. The pot's composition helps retain heat and distribute it evenly to the food during cooking. This thick-walled pot collects and slowly releases heat from the heating element, cooking food at a low temperature for a long time.

4. **The Lid**: The crockpot lid is usually glass or plastic and fits snugly over the top. It seals the pot to avoid evaporation and maintain cooking temperature. The transparent cover lets you monitor the cooking process without disturbing the pot's heat balance.

These elements create a perfect setting for slow cooking, where food is cooked at low heat for hours. Tender, delicious, and moist foods arise from this combination. How does the crockpot do this? Heat transfer physics and slow cooking chemistry explain it.

The Physics of Heat Transfer in a Crockpot

Heat transfer—the transport of thermal energy—is the foundation of slow cooking. When a crockpot's heating element is turned on, electrical energy becomes heat. Heat is transferred by conduction, convection, and radiation. While all three may contribute to cooking, conduction dominates crockpot heat transmission.

1. **Conduction**: Conduction happens in a crockpot when the heating element warms the inner pot, which heats the food. Heat from the heating element is uniformly distributed across the inner pot's thick ceramic or porcelain material. As the food in the pot heats up, its molecules vibrate faster, spreading heat. This moderate, consistent temperature rise cooks food evenly without scorching or drying it.

2. **Convection**: Convection is usually linked with liquids, but it also helps slow cook. The broth or sauce in the pot circulates heat around the meal as it heats up, helping to distribute it evenly. In slow-cooked stews and soups, liquid movement ensures that all ingredients are heated evenly.

3. **Radiation**: Radiation is a minor heat transfer method in a crockpot. In this style of cooking, slow, direct conduction is more significant than radiating heat from the heating element into the pot.

Conduction heat transmission allows the crockpot to maintain a steady temperature for slow, even cooking. This method produces delicate, delicious, and fully cooked food without continual supervision.

The Importance of Temperature Control

Temperature management is crucial to a crockpot. Crockpots cook food at a low, consistent temperature for a long time, unlike ovens and stovetops. Most crockpots have low and high settings. Some versions have a warm setting to keep food safe to serve without cooking.

1. **Low Setting**: The low setting of a crockpot maintains a temperature range of 170°F to 200°F (75°C to 93°C). Food cooks gradually at this low temperature for several hours, allowing flavors to develop and components to soften and amalgamate. Dishes that require extended cooking durations, such as stews, soups, and roasts, are suitable in this context.

2. **High Setting**: temperatures that were as high as 250°F (121°C). Even while it cooks food faster than low settings, this temperature is still far lower than traditional cooking methods. This option efficiently reduces cooking time without sacrificing the taste and softness that come with slow cooking.

3. **Warm Setting**: Recent versions feature a warming setting that maintains food at a safe serving temperature without further cooking. This maintains food temperature for an extended duration during potlucks and gatherings.

Effective temperature regulation in a crockpot is essential for achieving optimal results. The crockpot's temperature regulation ensures uniform and thorough cooking without desiccation or charring, whether you are making a tough cut of meat requiring many hours for tenderization or a rapid soup needing only a few hours.

Moisture Retention and the Role of the Lid

Crockpots efficiently preserve moisture owing to their lid configuration. Steam and moisture are contained by the pot's tight lid. During cooking, moisture from the ingredients evaporates and rises to the pot's lid, where it condenses. The dish self-bastes as condensation returns to it, preserving its moisture and flavor.

Slow-cooked dishes are soft and delicious owing to the regulated cooking conditions. Roasting or grilling, which eliminate moisture, can dehydrate or toughen food. Crockpots retain food moisture by sustaining humidity within the container.

The lid also regulates the pot's temperature. The sealed crockpot preserves heat from the heating element, which circulates and is absorbed by the food. This alleviates temperature variations and guarantees even frying on both sides.

The Chemistry of Slow Cooking

Slow cooking involves heat transfer, moisture retention, and chemical interactions that elevate the gastronomic experience. The prolonged cooking time and moderate temperature of a crockpot promote several chemical processes that improve the flavor, texture, and quality of the meal.

Collagen Breakdown

The breakdown of collagen, a protein present in bovine connective tissues, is an essential chemical reaction in slow cooking. Collagen is resilient and fibrous in its raw state; hence, tougher cuts of meat are less preferable when exposed to high-heat cooking methods. Extended exposure to low heat leads to the degradation of collagen into gelatin, yielding a soft texture in meat.

Slow cooking is efficacious for robust cuts like chuck roast, brisket, and pork shoulder because of this metamorphosis. These slices consist of collagen-dense connective tissue that retains its resilience and chewiness when exposed to high-temperature cooking. In a slow cooker, collagen progressively degrades over several hours, resulting in tender meat that can be readily separated with a fork.

Maillard Reaction

The Maillard reaction transpires when proteins and carbohydrates in food are exposed to elevated temperatures, leading to browning and the formation of intricate, delicious flavors. Crockpots can impede the Maillard reaction, typically linked to high-temperature grilling, roasting, or frying, especially during meat preparation.

While a crockpot does not reach the same temperatures as an oven or stovetop, its prolonged cooking time facilitates some browning, especially at the edges of the meat. The comprehensive Maillard reaction produces complex, nuanced flavors in slow-cooked meals.

Flavor Extraction and Blending

Slow cooking enhances the extraction and integration of flavors. Conventional cooking use high temperatures to swiftly produce flavors, frequently resulting in pronounced, distinct flavor profiles.

The prolonged cooking time in a crockpot systematically removes the tastes of herbs, spices, and other components. Incremental infusion amplifies the depth and taste of cuisine.

Crockpot stews allow veggies, meat, and seasonings to meld and enrich the broth with flavor over an extended duration. Over time, these flavors integrate, producing a more harmonic and balanced dish than if prepared quickly.

Enzyme Activity

Slow cooking preserves and activates enzymes that are destroyed at higher temperatures, as well as chemical processes including the Maillard reaction and collagen breakdown. These enzymes break down proteins and carbohydrates, improving flavor and texture.

At crockpot temperatures, vegetable enzymes break down complex carbs into simple sugars. This is why slow-cooked veggies taste sweeter than those cooked fast at higher temperatures. Enzymes make veggies soft and delicate, making them excellent for slow-cooked soups and stews.

The Importance of Time in Slow Cooking

Time matters as much as temperature in a crockpot. Prolonged cooking duration guarantees a thorough cooking procedure unattainable by expedited methods. Time facilitates the breakdown of resilient fibers, the development of intricate flavors, and the retention of moisture in slow cooking.

1. **Tenderizing Tough Cuts of Meat**: One of the best things about slow cooking is that it turns tough meat into tasty meals. Because they have connective tissue, cooking beef, hog shoulder, and chuck roast quickly at high temperatures can make them tough and chewy. When you cook these cuts at a low temperature for a long time, the connective tissue breaks down. This makes the meat soft and easy to shred.

2. **Flavor Development**: Longer cooking brings out the flavors more fully. If you cook garlic, onions, and spices slowly, their flavors will come out over a few hours. This will make the dish taste better and be more balanced. It takes time for stews and soups to blend the flavors of all the ingredients together.

3. **Moisture Retention**: Time also changes how well moisture is kept in. Food doesn't lose its wetness quickly when cooked at low temperatures in a crockpot. This is very important because

lean meat and vegetables can dry out quickly when the temperature rises. Slowly simmering these foods keeps their wetness in, which makes them soft and juicy.

Energy Efficiency of a Crockpot

Although slow cooking takes a long time, crockpots are energy efficient. The appliance's low wattage and lower cooking temperature than baking or frying make it efficient.

1. **Low Wattage**: On low, a normal crockpot needs 70–250 watts and on high, 300 watts. Baking or roasting in an oven uses 2000–3000 watts. A crockpot consumes much less energy than an oven even after cooking for several hours.

2. **Heat Retention**: Energy efficiency is also improved by crockpot design. The lid holds heat and moisture, so the crockpot uses less energy to maintain a steady temperature. This makes it great for long-cooking stews, roasts, and braises.

The combination of low wattage and efficient heat retention makes the crockpot an energy-efficient option for slow cooking, allowing you to prepare delicious meals without consuming large amounts of electricity.

Crockpot Cooking Tips and Common Misconceptions

A versatile and useful kitchen equipment, the crockpot has some popular misconceptions about how it works and how to use it. Understanding these myths will help you maximize your crockpot and make delicious dishes every time.

Misconception 1: You Can't Overcook Food in a Crockpot

A widespread misperception regarding crockpots is that the low temperature prevents overcooking. Although crockpots cook meals gently, they might overcook certain ingredients if left in the pot too long. If cooked too long, vegetables and meat can mush and dry out.

Follow recipe cooking times and use a timer or automatic shutoff to avoid overcooking. This keeps food from cooking after it's done, preserving texture and flavor.

Misconception 2: Crockpots Are Only Good for Soups and Stews

Another myth is that crockpots are only for soups, stews, and other liquid-heavy foods. Crockpots are great at these meals, but they can do more. Roasts, casseroles, desserts, and bread can be cooked in crockpots. These dishes work best when the cooking time and liquid content match the ingredients.

Use a little liquid when cooking a roast to keep it moist without making a stew. For cakes and breads, line the saucepan with parchment paper and cook on a lower heat to achieve equal cooking.

Misconception 3: Browning Meat Before Slow Cooking is Unnecessary

Browning meat before adding it to the slow cooker is common. Some home cooks ignore this step, thinking slow cooking will tenderize the meat. Browning meat before slow cooking adds flavor.

Before slow cooking, browning meat on the stovetop starts the Maillard process, which adds depth and rich tastes. The crockpot can mimic this reaction, although browning the meat at higher temps is better. Browning the meat before slow cooking improves taste and satisfaction.

Slow cooking with a crockpot involves intriguing heat transmission, moisture retention, and chemical reactions. Unlike shorter cooking methods, the crockpot tenderizes tough portions of meat and blends flavors by cooking at a low, consistent temperature for a long time. The crockpot is useful for home cooks who want to make hearty meals quickly because it saves energy, lets you control the temperature, and keeps the wetness in.

Knowing about the science and chemistry of a crockpot can help you make the most of its many uses and come up with new ways to cook. It's easy to make tasty and cozy foods like stews, roasts, and desserts in a crockpot.

CHAPTER 3:
Types of Crockpots and Their Features

Slow cookers, sometimes called crockpots, are essential appliances for any home because of their many uses and simplicity of use. They facilitate meal preparation without requiring supervision. As cooking demands have changed throughout time, crockpots have evolved to include a wider range of capabilities. Selecting a crockpot that suits your cooking preferences and style can be made easier by being aware of the many varieties and how they operate.

1. Basic Crockpots

There are a lot of features even the most basic crockpots. Their intended users are those who value simplicity and effectiveness over features that add unnecessary complexity.

Single Temperature Setting

There is typically just one temperature option on simpler crockpots, and that's either "Low" or "High." For those who prefer to let their food cook on their own without constantly checking the temperature, these models are ideal. Their slow-cooking capabilities make them ideal for soups, stews, and pot roasts.

Manual Controls

Standard models have user guides. A crockpot's on/off and temperature-setting controls are often located on a dial or switch. Despite lacking timers or user-configurable settings, these gadgets are popular due to their user-friendliness. Due to the absence of additional features, they are more affordable compared to other versions.

Durability and Ease of Use

Due to their sturdy construction and lack of electronic components, these crockpots are quite durable and seldom break. They're perfect for those who lack confidence in the kitchen or who simply prefer a less involved affair. For those who like to manually set the timer or are just starting out in the kitchen, their straightforward design is ideal.

2. Programmable Crockpots

This type of crockpot is more useful and gives cooks more control over their food. There are a lot of different ways to set these crockpots to cook and heat food.

Digital Timers

I love the digital timers on programmable crockpots. For certain varieties, customers can select a cooking time of 30 minutes to 24 hours. The crockpot automatically switches to "Keep Warm" mode once the meal is done cooking, ensuring its safety until it's time to serve. For those in a rush who would like a homemade meal, this is fantastic.

Multiple Temperature Settings

Many crockpots that are programmed feature more than two temperature settings. More temperature settings beyond just "Low" and "High" are available on several models. Even "Medium" or more precise settings are available on some. More varieties of dishes are made feasible by this. Enhanced control over temperature could be beneficial for delicate dishes like seafood and dairy preparations.

Preset Cooking Programs

Certain programmable crockpots are already capable of cooking stews, meats, and desserts. To achieve the finest outcomes, these systems instantly adjust the cooking temperature and time. Those who are unsure about how to prepare a dish or are new to cooking would benefit from this tool.

LCD Displays and Control Panels

Most programmable crockpots include LCD displays and simple controls. This panel shows remaining cooking time and temperature. The time, temperature, and cooking mode buttons on the control panel are usually obvious. Tech-savvy people who like hands-on cooking like these models.

Versatility in Meal Preparation

Programmable crockpots are popular with families that like to try new recipes. They can prepare soups, stews, baked items, and slow-cooked meats. Setting cooking times and temperatures ensures meals are cooked accurately and effectively, making them excellent for multitasking cooks or busy people.

3. Multi-Function Crockpots

The multi-function crockpot is an all-in-one kitchen appliance. Crockpots like this have several uses: slow cooking, sautéing, steaming, baking, and even pressure cooking. When it comes to cooking, they are the most practical and adaptable tools.

Multiple Cooking Modes

Compared to slow cookers, multi-function crockpots offer more cooking options. You can saute or sauté the meat in some crockpots before slow cooking it. By doing away with the need for extra pans, this cuts down on cleanup and saves time. With the ability to steam, roast, or pressure cook, these gadgets make it easy for home cooks to whip up a variety of recipes without breaking the bank.

Pressure Cooking Feature

The ability to combine slow cooking with pressure cooking speed is now included in many multi-function crockpots. Thanks to this, customers can whip up gourmet treats that would normally take hours in only a few minutes. Tenderizing meats and quickly preparing beans and grains are two of pressure cooking's best uses. These crockpots are perfect for small kitchens since they can replace pressure cookers.

Steaming and Baking Features

In addition to slow cooking and pressure cooking, multi-function crockpots also have the ability to steam and bake. The steaming function is great for making nutritious meals like steamed fish or vegetables. Bake a variety of delicious treats in the crockpot, including cakes, breads, and more. The multi-function model is perfect for individuals who enjoy experimenting with different recipes and cooking techniques.

Customizable Settings

Typically, multi-function crockpots have settings that can be adjusted. Cooking time and temperature can be adjusted by hand for each recipe. Yogurts and custards, which are delicate foods, require precise temperature control, which some varieties offer. With these crockpots, professional cooks may adjust every setting to their liking, giving them complete control over their dishes.

Pre-Programmed Meal Settings

Many multi-use crockpots have meal settings that automatically adjust the cooking time and temperature depending on the sort of food you're preparing. These presets take the guesswork out of cooking for newbies. Multiple meals can be prepared simultaneously using meats, stews, rice, and soups.

Energy Efficiency

Although they are versatile, numerous crockpots are energy efficient. There are numerous models available that consume less energy than traditional ovens and stovetops, allowing home chefs to contribute to environmental sustainability. The ability to make a variety of meals in one appliance reduces the need to run several kitchen machines, lowering household energy usage.

4. Smart Crockpots

Smart crockpots are a new option for chefs thanks to advances in technology. These models and gadgets, which are also called "home assistants," let people watch and control their cooking from afar.

Wi-Fi and Bluetooth Connectivity

Smart crockpots can be controlled via a smartphone application using Wi-Fi or Bluetooth. The application enables crockpot users to adjust the cooking time, temperature, and "Keep Warm" setting. This is advantageous for persons who are busy and may not be at home for meal preparation, nevertheless desire to guarantee that their food is properly cooked. Remote management of your crockpot can offer a sense of calm and avert the risks of overcooking or undercooking.

Voice-Control Integration

Smart crockpots frequently communicate with Amazon Alexa or Google Assistant. Users may employ voice commands to regulate their Crockpots. While your hands are occupied, you may request that Alexa establish a timetable or adjust the temperature. This hands-free motion simplifies multitasking in the kitchen.

App-Based Recipe Guides

Smart crockpots frequently include an app-based recipe guide that provides step-by-step instructions for a variety of dishes. By recommending culinary temperatures and times for a variety of recipes, these applications may assist in achieving consistent results. In certain applications, users are permitted to input ingredients and receive recipe recommendations that are created accordingly. This is an excellent alternative for home cooks who are uncertain about where to begin when attempting new cuisines.

Remote Monitoring and Adjustments

Smart crockpots offer the advantage of allowing you to monitor the culinary process from a distance. Monitor the temperature, determine the duration of heating, and receive notification when the food is prepared. Real-time monitoring ensures that meals are prepared to perfection without necessitating constant supervision. You may monitor your crockpot while conducting household tasks or working.

Advanced Programming Options

Compared to conventional crockpots, smart customizable crockpots enable the user to establish a greater number of options. Smart crockpots are capable of generating culinary plans that require more than one step. The crockpot can be programmed to commence cooking at a specific temperature and transition to a different temperature after a specified duration. This feature is particularly effective for recipes that require varying cooking temperatures, such as the slow cooking of flesh at a low temperature and the subsequent burning at a high temperature.

5. Portable Crockpots

Bringing food on trips, to family events, and to potlucks is easier when you have a portable crockpot. These versions are made to be portable and make delivering hot, already-cooked meals easier.

Locking Lids and Handles

Portable crockpots need lids that lock in place. Keeps the crockpot from spilling or leaking while it's being moved. The lid locks tightly, so food stays safe while it's being moved. A lot of movable crockpots have sturdy handles that make them easy to move from the kitchen to the car or an event.

Compact and Lightweight Design

Portable crockpots are smaller and lighter than regular ones. Smaller dishes are easier to travel and store and have a smaller capacity, making them ideal for smaller groups. Portable crockpots are perfect for on-the-go meal prep because they slow-cook like larger models.

Keep-Warm Features

The "Keep Warm" option on many portable crockpots keeps meals warm throughout transport. This is helpful when you need to bring a dinner to a party but aren't ready to serve it. The "Keep Warm" feature keeps your cuisine hot until serving.

Ideal for Tailgating and Potlucks

Portable crockpots are popular for tailgating, potlucks, and family events. These types are ideal for social events since they can convey hot meals without spilling. Portable crockpots make it easy to make and serve tasty dishes like slow-cooked chili and casseroles.

Each model of crockpot caters to different cooking needs and tastes. There's a crockpot for everyone, whether you like a basic one, a programmable one, a multi-function appliance, a smart one, or a travel-friendly one. Understanding the benefits of each type can help you choose the ideal one for your kitchen and lifestyle, making meal preparation easy and fun.

CHAPTER 4:
Crockpot Cooking Tips

Slow cooking, or crockpot cooking, is a popular and easy technique to cook. It lets stews, soups, and desserts boil gently for hours, allowing the ingredients to create deep, rich tastes. Slow cooking may seem simple, but there are dos and don'ts that may make or break a meal. Understanding these will assure tasty results.

Do: Use the Right Size Crockpot

It's crucial to choose the correct crockpot size for your recipe. 1.5- to 8-quart crockpots are common. The size should equal the amount of food you're cooking. Aim to fill your crockpot half to three-quarters full. Underfilling might cook the meal too rapidly, while overfilling can produce uneven cooking.

Side dishes and one- or two-person meals are best in a 1.5- to 3-quart crockpot. A 6 to 8-quart type is suitable for larger amounts when cooking for a family or group. Use the right size to cook food evenly and avoid spilling.

Don't: Lift the Lid While Cooking

One of the most typical crockpot blunders is lifting the lid to check on the meal. Every time the lid is lifted, heat escapes and takes 20–30 minutes to recover. Slow cooking is hands-off, and the lid keeps the pot warm. Unless adding ingredients later or verifying doneness, don't peek.

Do: Layer Ingredients Properly

Layering crockpot items affects how they cook. Root vegetables like carrots and potatoes should be placed at the bottom of the crockpot since heat originates from the bottom. Meats and soft veggies cook faster and should be on top. This evenly cooks ingredients and prevents overcooking.

Don't: Add Dairy Too Early

Milk, cream, cheese, and yogurt can curdle if added too early while cooking. For a smooth, creamy texture without curdling, add dairy products in the last 30–60 minutes of cooking. Some recipes advocate adding dairy after slow cooking, notably in soups or creamy sauces.

Do: Use Less Liquid

Water doesn't evaporate in crockpots since the lid stays on. Crockpot recipes can reduce fluids, unlike typical cooking methods that require water or broth to prevent dryness. The meal might become watery or flavorless with too much liquid. Compared to stovetop or oven recipes, reducing liquid by a third is safe.

Don't: Add Frozen Ingredients

Throwing frozen meats or veggies into the crockpot may seem easy, but it can cause uneven cooking and hazardous food. Slower cooking temperatures for frozen foods increase microbial growth. To cook frozen foods evenly and safely in the crockpot, defrost them beforehand.

Do: Brown Meat Before Slow Cooking

While not required, browning beef, pork, or chicken before putting to the crockpot improves taste and texture. A thick, caramelized crust adds variety to the flavor profile when meat is browned. It also seals in liquids, keeping meat tender and moist during slow cooking.

Don't: Overcook Vegetables

Zucchini, bell peppers, and spinach cook faster than root vegetables or meats. Early additions might cause mushy, overcooked veggies that lose flavor and texture. Adding delicate veggies in the last hour of cooking preserves their color, texture, and nutritional content.

Do: Use the Low Setting for Tender Results

Crockpots usually have two settings: low and high. Low and high settings are usually 200°F and 300°F, respectively. Both settings will eventually reach the same temperature, but cooking on low tenderizes meats and brings forth rich, deep tastes. When possible, utilize low for longer periods for best results. In a hurry, high heat may not yield the same delicate, melt-in-your-mouth feel as slow cooking on low.

Don't: Use Fresh Herbs Too Early

During long crockpot cooking, fresh herbs like basil, parsley, and cilantro lose flavor and color. Add fresh herbs at the end of cooking or before serving to optimize flavor. However, dried herbs can endure prolonged cooking and release their flavors gradually, so they can be added early.

Do: Adjust Seasonings at the End

Sometimes the flavors of some ingredients, especially salt and spices, are subdued by slow cooking. This is why it's a good idea to sample your dish as it's almost done and adjust the seasonings accordingly. To bring the tastes back to life, you might need to add a little extra salt, pepper, or herbs.

Don't: Cook Everything on High

Although it could be tempting to cook on high to expedite the process, this isn't always a good idea. Cooking food on high heat might result in overcooked veggies, harder meat cuts, and generally less tasty food. Patience is key when slow cooking, and the best results are frequently obtained by cooking food slowly and low. It's preferable to start cooking early rather than trying to speed the process up by increasing the heat if you're pressed for time.

Types of Crockpots and Their Features

There are many different kinds and sizes of crockpots available, and each one has special characteristics to meet a variety of cooking demands. It will be easier for you to select the ideal crockpot for your needs and cooking style if you are aware of the various varieties and their unique qualities. Below is a summary of some of the most prevalent varieties along with their attributes:

Manual Crockpots

Slow cookers that are operated manually are the most basic kind. Usually, they include a straightforward dial or switch with three basic settings to choose from: "low," "high," and "warm." For people who like a hassle-free cooking experience, these crockpots are simple and quick to use. Nevertheless, manual crockpots lack automated shut-off mechanisms and timers, so you will need to be present to switch them off after cooking is finished.

Programmable Crockpots

Better than manual models, programmable crockpots give you more control over the cooking process. These types have digital controls that let you program a precise temperature and cooking time. Many programmable crockpots will automatically move to the "warm" setting when the cooking time is up, maintaining a safe temperature for your meal until you're ready to serve. Those who want to set their crockpot in the morning and return home to a prepared meal at night will find this option especially useful.

Multi-Cookers

Multi-cookers are multipurpose kitchen tools that can be used as a rice cooker, crockpot, pressure cooker, and more. These appliances combine several cooking activities into one, which makes them perfect for individuals looking for an all-in-one cooking solution or for those with a small kitchen. Many preset cooking modes, including as sautéing, slow cooking, and pressure cooking, are commonly included in multi-cookers, providing a broad range of meal possibilities.

Travel Crockpots

These little crockpots are perfect for taking on the go. These are great for traveling because they have locking lids and handles that prevent spills. If you're hosting a dinner party, potluck, or family reunion, these are the way to go. Even more convenient are portable crockpots that come with dedicated carrying bags. You can keep food warm while traveling with a number of portable crockpots that offer a warm setting.

Crockpots with Temperature Probes

Some crockpots have a built-in temperature probe that lets you check the internal temperature of your food while it cooks. When cooking large portions of meat, such roasts or whole fowl, this feature is very helpful because it prevents the meat from overcooking and makes sure it reaches the right temperature. Once the food reaches the ideal internal temperature, the temperature probe will instantly turn off the stove, so you can rest easy knowing it's cooked to perfection.

Dual-Compartment Crockpots

Because of their independent cooking sections, dual-compartment crockpots enable the simultaneous cooking of two dishes. This works well for cooking two distinct foods at different temperatures or for cooking a main course and a side dish at the same time. Because each section usually has its own temperature control, you can adjust how long each food item cooks for. Double-chambered crockpots are perfect for entertaining or quickly and easily preparing an entire dinner.

Crockpots with Stovetop-Safe Inserts

Some crockpot models have detachable burner inserts that allow you to sauté or brown food before adding it to the slow cooker. Cooking is simplified by this function, which eliminates the need for extra pans. Usually made of metal or ceramic, these inserts are designed to withstand the extreme heat produced by the burner. Stovetop-safe inserts are ideal for browning meals, such as stews or braised meats, because they enhance the flavor of the food.

Crockpots with Delayed Start Timers

Slow cookers with delay-start timers enable the cooking process to be scheduled to begin at a specific time. This feature is useful for prepping ingredients without starting the cooking process right away. The delayed start timer, for instance, lets you set the crockpot to cook later in the morning so you may make your meal ahead of time and have it finished by midday. It is important to use caution while utilizing this capability when working with perishable foods, since prolonged exposure to room temperature before cooking could jeopardize food safety.

Wi-Fi-Enabled Crockpots

When a crockpot is Wi-Fi-enabled, it makes things easier because you can control the cooking process from your phone. As long as you have an internet connection, you can use this tool to start, stop, or change the cooking time and temperature from anywhere. This is especially helpful for busy people who want to keep an eye on and handle their slow cooker while they're not at home. Many crockpots that are connected to Wi-Fi come with extra features like recipe ideas and detailed cooking instructions, which makes planning dinner easier.

Eco-Friendly Crockpots

Crockpots designed for the environment prioritize energy efficiency. Slow cookers made of eco-friendly materials use less electricity than typical ones. Eco-friendly crockpots with energy-saving modes and solar panels use less power when cooking. If you value sustainability, an eco-friendly crockpot lets you slow cook while reducing your environmental effect.

Crockpots come in many varieties to suit different cooking demands. Everyone can use crockpots, from manual to WiFi-enabled. By studying the many types and their benefits, you may choose the best crockpot for your lifestyle and cooking style. With its convenience, variety, and energy efficiency, this crockpot makes slow cooking fun and easy.

CHAPTER 5:
Adapting Recipes for the Crockpot and is Benefits

The slow cooker, often known as a crockpot, has gained popularity in recent years because to the demand for convenience in contemporary cooking, stemming from individuals' busy schedules. Its ability to effortlessly convert mundane components into a delectable meal makes it appealing to numerous home cooks, especially those with demanding schedules. This chapter will examine the advantages of use a slow cooker and methods for modifying recipes accordingly.

Understanding the Crockpot Method

You need to know what slow cooking is and how it's different from other cooking techniques before you can modify recipes for the crockpot. A countertop crockpot with moist heat can cook food for extended lengths of time. Food can simmer for hours at 175°F (79°C) to 215°F (102°C) because to the low temperatures. This lengthy cooking technique dissipates odors, softens tough meat portions, and maintains nutritional value.

Cooking in a Crockpot is convenient. Your components can cook for hours while you take care of other tasks. When converting stovetop or oven recipes to crockpot dishes, it's frequently necessary to adjust the cooking times, temperatures, and ingredient combinations in order to achieve the desired texture and flavor.

Adapting Stovetop and Oven Recipes for the Crockpot

Although adapting traditional recipes for the slow cooker may seem like a breeze, it's crucial to understand how each component reacts in this appliance. Some factors to keep in mind while making changes to a crockpot recipe are:

Adjusting Liquid Levels

Reducing the liquid content is one of the first adjustments you'll need to make when modifying a recipe. Because of its sealed environment, the crockpot keeps moisture during cooking, unlike stovetop or oven cooking, where liquid evaporates during the process. Consequently, less liquid will be needed in the crockpot for recipes that rely on evaporation or reduction for thickness (such as soups and stews). Generally speaking, unless the dish is intended to be a soup or stew with a lot of stock, reduce the liquid by roughly one-third to one-half.

In recipes that call for exact thickness, like sauces or gravies, you might have to add more liquid at the end of cooking. This can be accomplished by adding a thickening ingredient, such as flour or cornstarch, or by taking off the lid to let some liquid evaporate.

Layering Ingredients

It also matters what order you put components in the crockpot, especially when modifying recipes for slow cooking. Foods put towards the bottom of the crockpot cook more quickly than those placed on top because heat rises from the bottom of the pot. Carrots, potatoes, and onions are examples of dense vegetables that should be added first. Meats and poultry are good examples of proteins; layer more delicate vegetables or items that cook quickly on top. By doing this, you can be sure that everything cooks through to the right tenderness and consistency.

Pre-Cooking for Better Flavor

Even though cooking in a crockpot is incredibly convenient, adding a few steps from traditional recipes will still improve flavor. To further improve the final dish's flavor, try browning the beef or sautéing the onions and garlic before adding them to the crockpot. Because of its low cooking temperature, the crockpot alone is not able to provide the caramelized coating of taste that this additional step creates.

This is a quick step to add, but it can make all the difference between a meal that is flavorless and one that is nuanced and full of depth.

Cooking Times and Temperature

Changing cooking periods is a key component of crockpot recipe adaptation. Meals that cook in the oven or on the stovetop for thirty minutes on average will take six to eight hours on the low setting or three to four hours on the high setting in the crockpot. The slow-cooking quality of a crockpot makes it perfect for recipes that require simmering; nevertheless, timing changes will be required to prevent overcooking certain ingredients, particularly delicate vegetables, fish, or dairy products like milk and cream.

To keep delicate ingredients from getting mushy or losing their flavor, add them during the last hour of cooking. Likewise, it's advisable to add dairy-containing ingredients last because prolonged heat exposure can cause them to curdle.

Seasoning and Spices

Another aspect of crockpot cooking that needs careful adjustment is seasoning. After slow cooking for several hours, herbs and spices may lose their power and have a more subdued flavor profile than when they are cooked over higher heat for a shorter period of time. To prevent overly bland meals, season with more salt before cooking and, if possible, taste as it cooks to make adjustments. Fresh herbs, such parsley or basil, added just before serving bring out the full taste.

The Benefits of Using a Crockpot

After discussing the process of modifying recipes for the crockpot, let us examine the numerous ways in which this versatile appliance can enhance your cookery.

Convenience and Time Management

Using a crockpot enables you to cook food without the need to continuously stir it. Once all of the ingredients have been collected and the crockpot's timer has been set, it will manage the remainder. Individuals who are employed for extended periods of time and have demanding families may find it advantageous to arrive home to a heated, pre-prepared meal. The crockpot allows you to do other things, such as go to work, conduct errands, or simply unwind at home, because it can operate unattended.

Furthermore, numerous crockpots are equipped with programmable features that enable you to specify precise cooking times and autonomously transition to warm mode upon the conclusion of the cycle. This guarantees that your meal will be prepared and served at the exact time you require it.

Cost Efficiency

Slow cooking has the potential to reduce costs in comparison to other culinary methods. The most effective method for tenderizing economical cuts of meat, including chicken thighs, swine shoulders, and chuck roast, is to cook them at a low temperature for an extended period of time. By cooking these cuts progressively, you can create delectable dishes that are both tender and flavorful at a low cost.

Another advantage of crockpots is their energy efficiency. Even when cooking for extended periods, crockpots consume significantly less energy than ovens. Consequently, it is a cost-effective alternative for individuals who wish to decrease their energy consumption without sacrificing the content of their meals.

Health Benefits

In more than one respect, the utilization of a crockpot encourages a nutritious cooking method. Initially, the nutrients are retained when food is cooked at low temperatures and at a sluggish pace. The moist heat of a crockpot is more effective at retaining the nutrients of vegetables than high-temperature frying or barbecuing.

Additionally, the utilization of whole, unprocessed ingredients is encouraged by the crockpot. By preparing your own meals at home, you can circumvent the harmful fats, preservatives, and added sodium that are frequently present in pre-packaged or takeout options. It is effortless to prepare nutritious, well-balanced meals by incorporating fresh vegetables, lean proteins, lentils, and whole grains.

Meal Planning and Batch Cooking

The utilization of a crockpot facilitates meal planning and mass preparation. This appliance is capable of preparing large quantities of food simultaneously, and it is simple to divide it out for future meals due to its substantial capacity. This is an excellent option for families or individuals who wish to prepare their meals a day or two in advance, allowing them to savor them throughout the week.

Chilis, casseroles, stews, and soups all benefit from bulk cooking in the crockpot. They are ideal for preparing in advance and subsequently reheating in the oven or freezer. This not only reduces food waste but also saves time by allowing remains to be transformed into alternative dishes.

Versatility

One additional benefit of crockpots is their adaptability. It is particularly adept at preparing thick soups and stews, but it is capable of preparing a wide range of foods, such as breakfast items such as oatmeal and frittatas, as well as desserts like cakes and puddings. Crockpot recipes are an excellent choice for those who wish to experiment with various cuisines without incurring excessive expenditures on new cookware due to their adaptability.

Making homemade stocks, sauces, and broths in the crockpot is an excellent method for reducing the consumption of processed, store-bought alternatives. By modifying slow cooker recipes, you can experiment with an infinite number of flavors and textures with minimal effort and time spent monitoring them.

Less Mess and Easy Cleanup

Meal preparation and washing are simplified through the utilization of a crockpot. The majority of meals are prepared in a single pot, eliminating the necessity for multiple pans, pots, or implements. Many crockpots are equipped with detachable components that can be cleaned in the dishwasher, which simplifies the cleaning process. This is a lifesaver if you prefer not to wash the dishes after a lengthy day.

The crockpot provides an extraordinary range of advantages for contemporary home cooking, including its exceptional adaptability in recipe adaptation and its exceptional simplicity of use. By making a few simple modifications, it is possible to transform your preferred stovetop or oven recipes into crockpot-friendly dishes without compromising any of the quality, nutrition, or flavor. The crockpot is an essential appliance that will simplify and increase productivity, regardless of whether your kitchen objectives include energy conservation, time savings, or the exploration of new culinary experiences.

BREAKFAST RECIPES

1. Seafood Eggs

- Servings: 4
- Cook: 2.5 Hours

Ingredients:

- 4. beaten eggs
- Cream cheese, 2 tbsp
- 1 tsp. of Italian herbs and spices
- 6 oz shrimps, peeled.
- 1 teaspoon olive oil

Directions:

1. Beat together cream cheese and eggs.
2. Add some Italian spice and shrimp.
3. After that, pour the egg mixture into the ramekins after lining them with olive oil.
4. You should put the ramekins in the slow cooker.
5. Warm the eggs for 2.5 hours on High.

Nutrition:

- 144 Kcal, 15.6g protein, 1.3g Carbs, 8.4g fat, 0g fiber

2. Kale Cups

- Servings: 4
- Cook: 2.5 Hours

Ingredients:

- 1 cup of finely chopped kale.
- Four eggs, lightly beaten.
- 1 tenth of a teaspoon of olive oil
- 1 teaspoon of ground chili peppers
- a half a cup of shredded Cheddar cheese

Directions:

1. Combine eggs, olive oil, and chili spice with the greens.
2. Spoon mixture into ramekins; sprinkle Cheddar cheese on top.
3. Place one ramekin in the slow cooker for each person.
4. Close the lid and cook the meal for 2.5 hours on high.

Nutrition:

- 140 Kcal, 9.6g protein, 2.6g Carbs, 10.3g fat, 0.5g fiber.

3. Bacon Potatoes

- Servings: 4
- Cook: 5 Hours

Ingredients:

- 4 potatoes with their skins on
- 1 teaspoon of thyme in its dry form
- Four tsp pure virgin olive oil
- 4 rashers of bacon

Directions:

1. Cut the potatoes in half, then drizzle with olive oil and dried thyme.
2. Next, split each slice of bacon in half.
3. Place the potatoes into the bowl of the Crock Pot and cover with slices of bacon.
4. Close the lid and cook on High for a total of five hours.

Nutrition:

- 290 Kcal, 10.6g protein, 33.9g Carbs, 12.8g fat, 5.2g fiber

4. *Squash Butter*

- Servings: 4
- Cook: 2 Hours

Ingredients:

- 1 cup butternut squash puree
- 1 teaspoon allspices
- 4 tablespoons applesauce
- 2 tablespoons butter
- 1 teaspoon corn flour

Directions:

1. Add all ingredients to the slow cooker and mix until well blended.
2. After that, replace the lid and cook the butter on High for two hours.
3. Place the cooked squash butter in the plastic container and allow it to thoroughly cool.

Nutrition:

- 78 Kcal, 0.2g protein, 6.3g Carbs, 5.8g fat, 0.8g fiber

5. *Ham Pockets*

- Servings: 4
- Cook: 1 Hour

Ingredients:

- 4 pita bread
- ½ cup of shredded cheddar cheese
- 4 ham slices

- Mayonnaise, one tablespoon
- 1 teaspoon dried dill

Directions:

1. Cheese, mayonnaise, and dill combine to form a delicious spread.
2. Next, tuck the ham and cheese slices inside the pita bread.
3. After wrapping the pitas in foil, put them in the Crock Pot.
4. For the entire hour, keep the heat on high.

Nutrition:

- 283 Kcal, 13.7g protein, 35.7g Carbs, 9.1g fat, 1.7g fiber,

6. Milk Pudding

- Servings: 2
- Cook: 7 Hours

Ingredients:

- a cup of milk
- 3 beaten eggs
- cornstarch, two tablespoons
- Vanilla extract, 1 teaspoon
- 1 tablespoon white sugar

Directions:

1. Beat together eggs, cornstarch, and milk.
2. Smooth out the mixture and stir in the vanilla essence and white sugar.
3. Once the liquid is added, replace the Crock Pot lid.
4. Reduce heat and cook for seven hours.

Nutrition:

- 214 Kcal, 12.3g protein, 20.1g Carbs, 9.1g fat, 9.7g fiber,

7. Peach Oats

- Servings: 3
- Cook: 7 Hours

Ingredients:

- 1/2 cup of rolled oats.
- One-and-a-half cups of milk
- 1/2 cup peaches, cut and pitted
- Cardamom, ground, one teaspoon

Directions:

5. You can use a slow cooker to prepare milk and steel-cut oats.
6. Add some peaches and ground cardamom to the mixture. Just give the ingredients a quick swirl, cover, and don't overwork them.
7. Cook for seven hours in your slow cooker.

Nutrition:

- 159 Kcal, 7g protein, 24.8g Carbs, 3.8g fat, 3.2g fiber

8. Leek Eggs

- Servings: 4
- Cook: 2.5 Hours

Ingredients:

- 10 oz leek, sliced.
- 4 eggs, beaten.
- 1 teaspoon olive oil
- ½ teaspoon cumin seeds
- 3 oz Cheddar cheese, shredded.

Directions:

1. Leek can be combined with eggs and olive oil.
2. Next, combine everything in a slow cooker.
3. To the beaten eggs, add a small amount of Cheddar cheese and cumin seeds.
4. Close the lid and cook on High for 2.5 hours.

Nutrition:

- 203 Kcal, 11.9g protein, 10.8g Carbs, 12.9g fat, 1.3g fiber

9. Raspberry Chia Porridge

- Servings: 4
- Cook: 4 Hours

Ingredients:

- Raspberries, around 1 cup's
- Add 3 tbsp. of maple syrup.
- 1 cup chia seeds
- 4 cups of milk

Directions:

1. In a slow cooker, simmer the milk and chia seeds on low for four hours.
2. Meanwhile, blend some raspberries with maple syrup until they're smooth.
3. Once the chia porridge is cooked, ladle it into individual bowls and garnish with the pureed raspberries.

Nutrition:

- 315 Kcal, 13.1g protein, 37.7g Carbs, 13.9g fat, 11.7g fiber,

10. Breakfast Monkey Bread

- Servings: 6
- Cook: 6 Hours

Ingredients:

- 10 oz biscuit rolls
- 1 tablespoon ground cardamom
- 1/4 cup honey.
- 2 tablespoons coconut oil
- 1 egg, beaten

Directions:

1. Roughly chop the cookie roll.
2. Stir in the ground cardamom and sugar.
3. The coconut oil should melt.
4. Place half of the chopped biscuit rolls in a single layer in the Crock Pot, then top with half of the ground cinnamon mixture and melted coconut oil.
5. Next, add the remaining biscuit roll chops on top, followed by a sprinkle of coconut oil and the cardamom mixture.
6. Next, cover the bread with the lid after brushing it with beaten egg.
7. Turn the heat to high and cook for six hours.
8. Make sure the bread is cooked through.

Nutrition:

- 178 Kcal, 6.1g protein, 26.4g Carbs, 7g fat, 2g fiber,

11. Omelet With Greens

- Servings: 2
- Cook: 2 Hours

Ingredients:

- 1/4 cup of milk 3 beaten eggs
- Baby arugula, 1 cup; arugula, diced; salt, 1/2 teaspoon.
- One Tablespoon of Avocado Oil

Directions:

1. Combine the eggs, milk, arugula, and salt in a bowl.
2. Pour some avocado oil inside the slow cooker.
3. After transferring the omelet egg mixture, cover the slow cooker.
4. On High, the dish should be cooked for two hours.

Nutrition:

- 115 Kcal, 9.6g protein, 2.5g Carbs, 7.6g fat, 0.3g fiber,

12. Coconut Oatmeal

- Servings: 6
- Cook: 5 Hours

Ingredients:

- Oatmeal, 2 cups
- 1.5 liters of coconut milk
- 1/2 liter of water
- 1 ounce of coconut flakes
- 2 tbsps. of honey

Directions:

1. Mix all ingredients together in a slow cooker and stir well.
2. After that, boil the oatmeal, covered, over low heat for five hours.

Nutrition:

- 313 Kcal, 5.4g protein, 25.8g Carbs, 22.5g fat, 4.8g fiber

13. Raspberry Chia Porridge

- Servings: 4
- Cook: 4 Hours

Ingredients:

- Raspberries, around 1 cup's
- Add 3 tbsp. of maple syrup.
- 1 cup chia seeds
- 4 cups of milk

Directions:

1. Simmer the milk and chia seeds for four hours on low heat in a slow cooker.
2. In the meantime, purée some raspberries in a blender with maple syrup.
3. After cooking, pour the chia porridge into individual bowls and top with the pureed raspberries.

Nutrition:

- 315 Kcal, 13.1g protein, 37.7g Carbs, 13.9g fat, 11.7g fiber

14. Breakfast Monkey Bread

- Servings: 6
- Cook: 6 Hours

Ingredients:

- 10 oz biscuit rolls
- 1 tablespoon ground cardamom
- 1/4 cup honey.
- 2 tablespoons coconut oil
- 1 egg, beaten

Directions:

1. Chop the cookie roll coarsely.
2. Add the sugar and ground cardamom and stir.
3. It should melt the coconut oil.
4. Spoon half of the chopped biscuit rolls into a single layer in the Crock Pot, and then sprinkle the remaining half with the melted coconut oil and crushed cinnamon mixture.
5. After that, place the remaining biscuit roll chops on top and scatter the cardamom mixture and coconut oil on top.
6. After coating the bread with beaten egg, replace the lid.
7. After adjusting the heat to high, cook for six hours.
8. Verify that the bread is thoroughly cooked.

Nutrition:

- 178 Kcal, 6.1g protein, 26.4g Carbs, 7g fat, 2g fiber, 27mg

15. Omelet With Greens

- Servings: 2
- Cook: 2 Hours

Ingredients:

- 1/4 cup of milk 3 beaten eggs
- Baby arugula, 1 cup; arugula, diced; salt, 1/2 teaspoon.
- One Tablespoon of Avocado Oil

Directions:

1. In a bowl, mix the eggs, milk, arugula, and salt.
2. Add a small amount of avocado oil to the slow cooker.
3. Once the omelet egg mixture has been transferred, place a lid on the slow cooker.
4. The dish should cook for two hours on High.

Nutrition:

- 115 Kcal, 9.6g protein, 2.5g Carbs, 7.6g fat, 0.3g fiber,

16. Coconut Oatmeal

- Servings: 6
- Cook: 5 Hours

Ingredients:

- Oatmeal, 2 cups
- 1.5 liters of coconut milk
- 1/2 liter of water
- 1 ounce of coconut flakes
- 2 tbsps. of honey

Directions:

1. In a slow cooker, combine all ingredients and stir thoroughly.
2. The oats should then be boiled for five hours over low heat, covered.

Nutrition:

- 313 Kcal, 5.4g protein, 25.8g Carbs, 22.5g fat, 4.8g fiber.

17. Olive Eggs

- Servings: 4
- Cook: 2 Hours

Ingredients:

- 10 kalamata olives, sliced
- 8 eggs, beaten
- 1 cayenne pepper teaspoon
- 1 tablespoon butter

Directions:

1. Grease the Crock Pot's bottom with butter.
2. Next, add the beaten eggs and cayenne pepper.
3. After that, place the olives on top of the eggs in the pan.
4. For two hours, cook the eggs on high.

Nutrition:

- 165 Kcal, 11.2g protein, 1.6g Carbs, 12.9g fat, 0.5g fiber.

18. Baby Carrots In Syrup

- Servings: 5
- Cook: 7 Hours

Ingredients:

- Baby carrots, 3 cups
- apple juice, 1 cup.
- Two tablespoons of brown sugar
- Vanilla extract, 1 teaspoon

Directions:

1. Combine vanilla essence, brown sugar, and apple juice.
2. Fill the Crock Pot with the liquid.
3. Cover the pan once the carrots are little.
4. Reduce the heat and cook for seven hours.

Nutrition:

- 81 Kcal, 0g protein, 18.8g Carbs, 0.1g fat, 3.7g fiber.

19.   Olive Eggs

- Servings: 4
- Cook: 2 Hours

Ingredients:

- 10 kalamata olives, sliced
- 8 eggs, beaten
- 1 cayenne pepper teaspoon
- 1 tablespoon butter

Directions:

1. Apply butter to lubricate the base of the Crock Pot.
2. Subsequently, incorporate cayenne pepper and beaten eggs.
3. Subsequently, place the olives atop the eggs and cover the pan.
4. Prepare the eggs at High temperature for a duration of 2 hours.

Nutrition:

- 165 Kcal, 11.2g protein, 1.6g Carbs, 12.9g fat, 0.5g fiber,

20. Baby Carrots In Syrup

- Servings: 5
- Cook: 7 Hours

Ingredients:

- Baby carrots, 3 cups
- apple juice, 1 cup.
- Two tablespoons of brown sugar
- Vanilla extract, 1 teaspoon

Directions:

1. Mix apple juice, brown sugar, and vanilla essence.
2. Pour the liquid into the Crock Pot.
3. When the carrots are little, cover the pan.
4. Reduce the heat and cook for seven hours.

Nutrition:

- 81 Kcal, 0g protein, 18.8g Carbs, 0.1g fat, 3.7g fiber,

21. Sweet Quinoa

- Servings: 4
- Cook: 3 Hours

Ingredients:

- quinoa, 1cup
- 3 cups of water
- 1/4 cup chopped dates.
- 1 diced apricot and 1/2 teaspoon nutmeg

Directions:

1. Place the dates, quinoa, and apricot into the Crock Pot.
2. Mix the mixture after adding the ground nutmeg.
3. Simmer it for three hours on high.

Nutrition:

- 194 Kcal, 6.4g protein, 36.7g Carbs, 2.8g fat, 4.1g fiber,

22. Broccoli Egg Casserole

- Servings: 5
- Cook: 3 Hours

Ingredients:

- beaten 4 eggs, 1/2 cup full-fat milk
- Melted 3 tablespoons of grass-fed butter Chop 1 1/2 cups of broccoli florets.
- pepper and salt as desired

Directions:

1. Whisk the eggs and milk together in a mixing bowl.
2. Grease the bottom of the Crockpot with melted butter.
3. Put the egg mixture and broccoli florets into the Crockpot.
4. Season the food with salt and pepper to taste.
5. Cover the pan and cook for 2 hours on high or 3 hours on low.

Nutrition:

- Kcal: 217; Carbs:4.6 g; Protein: 11.6g; Fat: 16.5g

23. Cream Grits

- Servings: 2
- Cook: 5 Hours

Ingredients:

- grits, 1/2 cup
- 1.5 cups thick cream
- water, 1 cup
- 1/fourth cup cream cheese

Directions:

1. Add the heavy cream, water, and grits to the Crock Pot.
2. Reduce the heat and cook the dish for 5 hours.
3. After the grits are cooked through, gently mix in the cream cheese.
4. Arrange the food in the serving bowls.

Nutrition:

- 151 Kcal, 1.6g protein, 6.9g Carbs, 13.2g fat, 1g fiber,

24. Egg Scramble

- Servings: 4
- Cook: 2.5 Hours

Ingredients:

- 4 eggs, beaten
- 1 tbspn butter, melted
- 2 oz Cheddar cheese, shredded

- ¼ teaspoon cayenne pepper
- 1 teaspoon ground paprika

Directions:

1. Beat eggs with cheese, butter, ground paprika, and cayenne.
2. Next, fill the Crock Pot with the mixture and cover it.
3. Cook on high for 2 hours.
4. Take off the top and scramble the eggs.
5. Close the lid and cook on high for 30 minutes.

Nutrition:

- 147 Kcal, 9.2g protein, 0.9g Carbs, 12g fat, 0.2g fiber,

25. *Crockpot Fisherman's Eggs*

- Servings: 2
- Cook: 3 Hours

Ingredients:

- 1 can organic sardines in olive oil
- 2 organic eggs
- ½ cup arugula, rinsed and drained
- ½ of artichoke hearts, chopped
- pepper and salt as desired

Directions:

1. Place the sardines in the bottom of the Crockpot.
2. Crack the eggs on top of the sardines and add the artichokes and arugula.
3. Season the food with salt and pepper to taste.
4. Cover the pan and cook for 2 hours on high or 3 hours on low.

Nutrition:

- Info Kcal :315; Carbs: 3.5g; Protein: 28g; Fat:20.6 g;

LUNCH RECIPES

26. *Lemon Garlic Dump Chicken*

- Serves: 6
- Prep: 9 minutes
- Cook: 8 hours

Ingredients

- 1/4 cup olive oil
- 2 tsp finely chopped garlic
- 6 boneless breasts of chicken
- 2 tablespoons of freshly squeezed lemon juice and 1 tablespoon minced parsley

Instructions

1. In a skillet over medium heat, warm the oil.
2. Garlic becomes golden brown when sautéed.
3. Put the chicken breasts in the slow cooker.
4. Drizzle with the garlic-scented oil.
5. Add the lemon juice and parsley. Pour in the water.
6. Cook for 8 hours on low or 6 hours on high, with the cover securely on.

Nutrition:

- 581; Carbs: 0.7g; Protein: 60.5g; Fat: 35.8g; Sugar: 0g; Fiber: 0.3g

27. *Harissa Chicken Breasts*

- Serves: 6
- Prep: 3 minutes
- Cook: 8 hours

Ingredients

- Olive oil, 1 tbsp
- 1 pound of skinless, boneless chicken breasts

- Salt as desired
- 2 tablespoons of Sriracha or Harissa sauce
- Toasted sesame seeds, 2 teaspoons

Instructions

1. Fill the crockpot with oil.
2. Once the chicken breasts are lined up, season with salt and pepper according to your taste.
3. Add the Sriracha or Harissa sauce and stir. Toss to ensure all ingredients are well combined.
4. Cook for 8 hours on low or 6 hours on high, with the cover securely on.
5. Top with toasted sesame seeds after cooking.

Nutrition:

- Kcal : 167; Carbs: 1.1g; Protein: 16.3g; Fiber: 0.6g

28. *Easy Crockpot Pulled Pork*

- Serves: 4
- Prep: 3 minutes
- Cook: 12 hours

Ingredients

- 4 pork shoulders that have been defatted.
- 1 thinly sliced little onion
- pepper and salt as desired
- one water cup
- one tablespoon rosemary

Instructions

1. Add all the ingredients to the slow cooker.
2. Simmer for eight hours on high or twelve hours on low.
3. Once cooked, shred the meat with forks.

Nutrition:

- 533; Carbs: 2g; Protein: 47.2g; Fat: 32.3g; Fiber: 1.4g

29. Asian Sesame Chicken

- Serves: 12
- Prep: 3 minutes
- Cook: 8 hours

Ingredients

- 12 chicken thighs with the skin and bones removed.
- 3 tablespoons water
- 2 tablespoons sesame oil
- 3.5 tbsp. soy sauce
- 1 finely sliced thumb-sized ginger

Instructions

1. Add all the ingredients to the slow cooker.
2. Combine all of the ingredients.
3. Cook for 8 hours on low or 6 hours on high, with the cover securely on.
4. Once cooked, garnish with toasted sesame seeds.

Nutrition:

- 458; Carbs: 1.5g; Protein: 32.2g; Fat: 35.05g; Fiber: 0.4g

30. *Cheesy Pork Casserole*

- Serves: 4
- Prep: 5 minutes
- Cook: 10 hours

Ingredients

- 4 sliced and bone-free pork chops
- 1 head of cauliflower, divided into florets.
- Chicken broth, one cup
- one tablespoon rosemary
- Cheddar cheese, two cups

Instructions

1. To the slow cooker, add the cauliflower florets and the pieces of pork chop.
2. Add the rosemary and chicken broth. Add salt and pepper to taste when preparing the meal.
3. Top with a little cheddar cheese.
4. Cook for 10 hours on low, covered.

Nutrition:

- 417; Carbs: 7g; Protein: 32.1g; Fat: 26.2g; Fiber: 5.3g

31. Bacon-Wrapped Pork Tenderloin

- Serves: 4
- Prep: 5 minutes
- Cook: 10 hours

Ingredients

- Pork tenderloin weighing 1 lb.
- pepper and salt as desired
- 1 teaspoon rosemary leaves
- 3 bacon slices, cut in half lengthwise.
- 2 tablespoons butter, melted

Instructions

1. To taste, add salt and pepper to the pork tenderloin.
2. After massaging, sprinkle the meat with the rosemary.
3. Place chunks of bacon all over the pork.
4. Use a generous amount of butter.
5. Place inside the slow cooker and cook for 10 hours on low or 8 hours on high.

Nutrition:

- Kcal : 401; Carbs: 1g; Protein: 38.5g; Fiber: 0.7g

32. Turkey with Zucchini

- Serves: 4
- Prep: 3 minutes
- Cook: 8 hours

Ingredients

- 1 lb. of ground turkey
- Striped, red peppers from two

- pepper and salt as desired
- 2 sliced green onions.
- 1 big, sliced zucchini

Instructions

1. To the Crockpot, add the red peppers and ground turkey.
2. Add salt and pepper to taste when preparing the meal.
3. Cook for 8 hours on low or 6 hours on high, with the cover securely on.
4. Add the green onions and zucchini 1 hour before the cook is done.
5. Simmer the veggies for a few more minutes, or until they are tender.

Nutrition:

- Kcal: 195; Carbs: 5.7g; Protein: 23.9g; Fat: 9.01g; Fiber: 2.5g

33. *Salmon with Lime Butter*

- Serves: 4
- Prep: 3 minutes
- Cook: 4 hours

Ingredients

- Salmon fillet, 1 pound, divided into 4 parts
- 1 teaspoon melted butter
- pepper and salt as desired
- 2 tablespoons of lime juice
- 1/2 teaspoon of grated lime zest

Instructions

1. Place all the ingredients into the slow cooker.
2. Shut the lid.
3. Simmer for two hours on high and four hours on low.

Nutrition:

- Kcal : 206; Carbs: 1.8g; Protein:23.7 g; Fiber: 0.5g

34. *Cilantro Lime Chicken*

- Serves: 3
- Prep: 3 minutes
- Cook: 8 hours

Ingredients

- 3 chicken breasts, bones and skin removed
- Juice from 3 limes, freshly squeezed
- minced 6 garlic cloves, 1 teaspoon cumin.
- ¼ cup cilantro

Instructions

1. Add all the ingredients to the slow cooker.
2. Mix everything together with a stir.
3. Cook for 8 hours on low or 6 hours on high, with the cover securely on.

Nutrition:

- Kcal: 522; Carbs: 6.1g; Protein: 61.8g; Fat: 27.1g; Fiber: 1.2g

35. *Spicy Curried Shrimps*

- Serves: 4
- Prep: 3 minutes
- Cook: 2 hours

Ingredients

- 1 1/2 pounds of deveined and shelled shrimp
- 1 tablespoon melted ghee or butter

- 1/fourth cup curry powder
- 1 cayenne pepper teaspoon
- pepper and salt as desired

Instructions

1. Add all the ingredients to the slow cooker.
2. Toss to fully combine all ingredients.
3. Put the lid on and cook on high for 30 minutes or low for 2 hours.

Nutrition:

- Kcal: 207; Carbs:2.2 g; Protein: 35.2g; Fat: 10.5g.

36. *Jalapeno Basil Pork Chops*

- Serves: 4
- Prep: 3 minutes
- Cook: 12 hours

Ingredients

- ½ cup jalapeno peppers, chopped
- 4 pork loin, chopped
- ½ cup dry white wine
- ¼ cup fresh basil
- To taste, add salt and pepper.

Instructions

1. In the crockpot, combine all the ingredients.
2. It's essential to thoroughly combine the ingredients.
3. Cook on high for 8 hours or on low for 12 hours.

Nutrition:

- Kcal: 472; Carbs: 6.1g; Protein: 38.2g; Fat:29.1 g; Fiber: 4.3g

37. Crockpot Pork Adobo

- Serves: 2
- Prep: 3 minutes
- Cook: 12 hours

Ingredients

- ¼ cup of soy sauce
- Apple cider vinegar, 4 tablespoons
- 1 pound of chopped pork loin
- Bay leaf, one
- Peppercorns, whole, 1 teaspoon

Instructions

1. Add all the ingredients to the slow cooker.
2. Stir until all ingredients are properly combined.
3. Simmer for eight hours on high or twelve hours on low.

Nutrition:

- Kcal : 328; Carbs: 3.21g; Protein: 53.84g; Fiber: 0.7g

38. One Pot Pork Chops

- Serves: 6
- Prep: 3 minutes
- Cook: 10 hours

Ingredients

- 6 chops of pork
- 200 grams of broccoli florets
- green and red bell peppers, 1/2 cup
- 1 sliced onion

- pepper and salt as desired

Instructions

1. Add all the ingredients to the slow cooker.
2. Mix everything together with a stir.
3. Once the lid is closed, cook for 10 hours on low or 8 hours on high.

Nutrition:

- Kcal : 496; Carbs: 6g; Protein: 37.1g; Fiber: 4.3g

39. *Salmon with Green Peppercorn Sauce*

- Serves: 4
- Prep: 5 minutes
- Cook: 3 hours

Ingredients

- Salmon fillets weighing 1 1/4 pounds, skin removed, divided into 4 parts
- pepper and salt as desired
- Unsalted butter, 4 tablespoons
- Lemon juice, 1/4 cup.
- vinegar and one teaspoon of green peppercorns

Instructions

1. To taste, add more salt and pepper to the salmon fillets.
2. Heat the butter in a skillet before searing the salmon fillets for two minutes on each side.
3. Place in a slow cooker and mix in the green peppercorns and lemon juice.
4. To adjust the seasoning, taste and adjust the amount of salt or pepper added to the dish.
5. Cook, covered, for an hour on high or three hours on low heat.

Nutrition:

- Kcal: 255; Carbs: 2.3g; Protein: 37.4g; Fat: 13.5g; Fiber: 1.5g

DINNER RECIPES

40. CrockPot Beef Picadillo

- Serves: 8
- Cook Time: 10 hr.

Ingredients

- crushed beef 2 pounds
- 20 green olives, pitted and diced
- 8 cloves of garlic, minced
- Enough pepper & salt
- 1 ½ tablespoons chile powder.
- 2 tablespoons dry oregano
- 1 teaspoon of powdered cinnamon.
- 1 cup sliced tomatoes, 1 chopped red onion, 2 diced Anaheim peppers with seeds

Directions:

1. Place all ingredients into the slow cooker.
2. Stir everything well.
3. Cook, covered, over high heat for 8 hours or low heat for 10 hours.

Nutrition Info:

- KCal: 317; Carbs: 4.5g; Protein: 29.6g; Fat: 19.8g

41. Cheesy Ranch Chicken

- Serves: 6
- Prep Time: 5 min.

- Cook Time: 8 hr.

Ingredients

- chicken breasts, bones removed 1 ¼ pounds
- sugar-free ranch dressing ½ C.
- ½ C. cheddar cheese, shredded
- ½ C. parmesan cheese, shredded
- Cayenne pepper to taste

Directions:

1. Add the ranch dressing to the slow cooker.
2. Put the chicken on top, as indicated.
3. For taste, add some spicy pepper flakes.
4. Add the two cheeses on top.
5. Close the lid and cook on low for 8 hours or on high for 6 hours.

Nutrition Info:

- KCal: 267; Carbs: 7g; Protein: 25g; Fat: 15.1g

42. Classic Pork Adobo

- Serves: 6
- Cook Time: 12 hr.

Ingredients

- 2 pounds pork chops, sliced
- garlic, minced 4 cloves
- 1 onion, diced
- 2 bay leaves
- ¼ C. soy sauce
- ½ C. lemon juice, freshly squeezed
- 4 quail eggs, boiled and stripped

Directions:

1. Place all the ingredients in the slow cooker, excluding the quail eggs.
2. Stir everything well.
3. Close the lid and cook on high for 10 hours or on low for 12 hours.
4. Add the quail eggs one hour before to the Cook Time expiring.

Nutrition Info:

- KCal: 371; Carbs: 6.4g; Protein: 40.7g; Fat: 24.1g

43. CrockPot Gingered Pork Stew

- Serves: 9
- Cook Time: 12 hr.

Ingredients

- crushed cinnamon 2 tbsp.
- crushed ginger 2 tbsp.
- 3 pounds pork shoulder, cut into cubes
- 2 C. homemade chicken broth
- Enough pepper & salt
- 1 tbsp. crushed allspice
- crushed cloves 1 ½ tsp.
- crushed nutmeg 1 tbsp.
- 1 tbsp. paprika

Directions:

1. Place all ingredients into the slow cooker.
2. Stir everything well.
3. Close the lid and cook on high for 10 hours or on low for 12 hours.

Nutrition Info:

- KCal: 425; Carbs: 4.2g; Protein: 38.7g; Fat: 27.4g

44. Popeye's Turkey Soup

- Serves 8

Ingredients

- 2 C. low-sodium chicken stock
- 1 teaspoon of black pepper
- Extra virgin olive oil
- 1 tsp. rosemary
- 1 turkey breast (2.5 pounds)
- 6 C. spinach, diced
- Diced 1 medium onion.
- 4 grated garlic cloves
- ½ tsp. thyme
- 1 tsp. salt

Directions

1. After sprinkling extra virgin olive oil on it, adjust the slow cooker to medium.
2. Cube the turkey breast into ½-inch pieces.
3. Heat 4 tablespoons of extra virgin olive oil in a skillet to brown the turkey breast.
4. With the turkey breast, spinach, onion, garlic, chicken stock, rosemary, thyme, salt, and pepper, cover and cook on low for eight hours.
5. Simmer it for four hours.

Nutrition Info:

- KCal 193, Fat 6 g, Carbs 8.8 g, Protein 25 g

45. Silky Broccoli and Cheese Soup

- Serves 8

Ingredients

- 1 teaspoon of black pepper
- Extra virgin olive oil
- 4 tbsp. ghee
- 3 C. broccoli florets
- cashews, soaked overnight, diced ½ C.
- cheddar, grated ½ C.
- 2 cups low-sodium chicken stock
- 1 C. coconut cream
- 1 tsp. coconut flour
- salt 1 tsp.

Directions

1. In a skillet, melt the ghee over medium heat.
2. Immediately stir in coconut flour in skillet.
3. Stir in coconut cream, process until smooth, and reserve.
4. Turn the slow cooker on to high and drizzle with extra virgin olive oil.
5. Add broccoli, cashews, salt, and black pepper to a slow cooker along with chicken stock. Mix well and cover to rest for ten minutes.
6. Cook for three hours while mixing the cheese and coconut cream combination.

Nutrition Info:

- KCal 216, Fat 20 g, Carbs 7 g, Protein 5 g

46. *Three-Bean Vegan Chili*

- Serves 4

Ingredients

- 15.5 oz can of kidney beans, ½
- 1/4 can (15.5 oz) of chickpeas
- Leaves of fresh cilantro, optional
- Vegetable oil, 2 tablespoons
- Diced tomatoes from ½ (28-oz) can
- 1-tablespoon chili powder
- 1 teaspoon ground cumin
- 1 teaspoon dried oregano
- 2 TBC of tomato paste
- 1 ¾ C. water
- ½ (15.5-oz.) can black beans
- 1 onion, finely diced
- 1 red bell pepper, chopped finely
- 1 green bell pepper, chopped finely
- 1 chopped and seeded jalapeño pepper
- 2 cloves garlic, minced
- ¼ tsp. salt

Directions

1. Coat the interior of a 6-quart slow cooker with oil. Add the minced garlic, diced onion, bell peppers, jalapeño, and a small amount of salt. Add the water, chili powder, cumin, oregano, tomato paste, and diced tomatoes.
2. Simmer for four hours on LOW heat with a lid on.
3. Before adding the beans to the slow cooker and combining them, they need to be drained and rinsed. Cover and continue cooking for a further two to four hours.
4. Add cilantro on the top of each serving.

Nutrition Info:

- KCal 245, Fat 2.9 g, Carbs 45.1 g, Protein 12.9 g

47. Beef Tomato Lentil Soup

- Serves 6-8

Ingredients

- 10 cherry tomatoes, to garnish
- Enough pepper & salt
- 2 pounds crushed beef
- ¼ C. prepared yellow mustard
- ¼ C. sour cream, to garnish
- ½ C. chopped green bell pepper
- ½ C chopped red bell pepper
- 6 C. beef stock
- 2 C. dry green lentils
- ½ C. creamed corn
- 1 (28-oz.) can diced tomatoes

Directions

1. In a frying pan, brown the ground beef and then drain the fat. Add the lentils, stock, mustard, green and red bell peppers, corn, and tinned tomatoes to the slow cooker.
2. Either cook for one hour and fifteen minutes on high or three hours and fifteen minutes on low. Sour cream and cherry tomatoes create a beautiful garnish.

Nutrition Info:

- KCal 299, Fat 11 g, Carbs 29 g, Protein 26.6 g

48. Spicy Pork with Mapo Tofu

- Serves: 2
- Cook Time: 8 hr.

Ingredients

- 1 jalapeno, sliced
- 4 garlic cloves, sliced
- 1 tsp. Sichuan peppercorns
- 2 C. chicken broth
- 2 tbsp. vegetable oil
- 8 oz. crushed pork
- 1 ½-inch ginger, grated
- 1 tbsp. tomato paste
- 1-pound silken tofu, drained and cubed

Directions:

1. In a skillet over medium heat with oil, render the crumbled pork for three minutes, swirling constantly.
2. Put everything in the CrockPot with the beef, excluding the silken tofu.
3. Mix thoroughly.
4. Close the lid and cook for 6 hours on high or 8 hours on low.
5. One hour before to the Cook Time expiring, add the tofu cubes.

Nutrition Info:

- KCal:372; Carbs: 5.3g; Protein:30.3 g; Fat: 25.8g

49. Coconut Turmeric Chicken

- Serves: 8
- Cook Time: 8 hr.

Ingredients

- 2-inch chunk of grated fresh ginger
- 4 cloves of garlic, grated
- Enough pepper & salt
- 1 whole chicken, cut into pieces
- ½ C. coconut milk, unsweetened
- 2 inch-knob fresh turmeric, grated

Directions:

1. Everything should be placed inside the Crock-Pot.
2. Cook on high heat for 6 hours or on low heat for 8 hours, covered.
3. Chop up some onions and add them on top.

Nutrition Info:

- KCal: 270; Carbs: 4.2g; Protein:24.5g; Fat: 18.9g; Fiber: 1.6g

50. CrockPot Beef Rendang

- Serves: 8
- Cook Time: 10 hr.

Ingredients

- ½ C. desiccated coconut, toasted
- 1 tsp. salt
- 6 cloves of garlic, minced
- 1 C. coconut cream
- 1 beef shoulder, cut into chunks
- ½ C. cilantro leaves, diced
- ½ C. water
- 1 tbsp. coconut oil
- 6 dried birds eye chilies, diced
- 1 tsp. crushed cumin

- 2 tsp. crushed coriander
- 1 tsp. turmeric powder
- 6 kafir lime leaves
- 2 stalks lemon grass

Directions:

1. Everything save the cilantro leaves should go into the slow cooker.
2. Stir everything well.
3. Cook, covered, over high heat for 8 hours or low heat for 10 hours.
4. When cooked, sprinkle cilantro on top.

Nutrition Info:

- KCal:305; Carbs: 6.5g; Protein: 32.3g; Fat: 18.7g

51. *Citrus infused Chicken Breasts*

- Serves 2-4

Ingredients

- 1 tbsp. of lemon pepper seasoning
- Salt and pepper
- Cooking spray
- Water
- 1 can cream of chicken soup
- Juice of half a lemon
- 2 large oranges, 1 juiced, 1 sliced
- 4 boneless and skinless chicken breasts

Directions

1. Coat the slow cooker's bottom with cooking spray.
2. Season the chicken breasts with salt and pepper.

3. Place the orange slices in the bottom of the slow cooker. The oranges should be positioned over the chicken breasts.
4. Before serving, mix in some lemon juice, orange juice, and lemon pepper to the soup.
5. Stir in half of a can of water. To guarantee a smooth finish, we suggest whisking the mixture.
6. Combine it with the chicken in the slow cooker.
7. Three hours on HIGH or six hours on LOW are needed for preparation.
8. Serve with your choice of greens and rice.

Nutrition Info:

- KCal 670, Fat 37.07 g, Carbs 34.52 g, Protein 45.31 g

52. *Butternut Squash Soup*

- Serves 2 (refrigerate leftovers)

Ingredients

- 5 C. butternut squash, cubed
- Enough pepper & salt
- ¼ C. heavy cream, optional
- 1 pinch freshly crushed nutmeg
- Water, about 3 C. or veggie stock
- 2 cloves garlic
- 1 small onion, diced

Directions

1. Transfer the onion, garlic, and squash to the slow cooker. Cover with enough water or vegetable stock. Add as much pepper and salt as desired. Stir well after adding the nutmeg.
2. Set it for 1-2 hours on HIGH or 3-5 hours on LOW.
3. Use an immersion blender to smooth up the soup once the squash is soft enough to mash.
4. For a creamier soup, add the heavy cream, if used, in the last half-hour of cooking. Stir the ingredients to combine them.
5. Taste it and adjust the seasoning with salt, pepper, and nutmeg if desired.
6. Hastily prepare and serve.

Nutrition Info:

- KCal 187, Fat 0.2 g, Carbs 43 g, Protein 10 g

53. *Homey Tomato Soup*

- Serves 4

Ingredients

- 1 sliced red pepper
- 1 teaspoon of oregano
- 1 teaspoon of basil
- 28 oz. diced tomatoes, canned, drained and rinsed
- 4 C. vegetable stock
- ½ C. cashews, soaked
- ½ C. sundried tomatoes
- 4 minced garlic cloves and a tsp of red pepper flakes
- Add pepper and salt.
- 8 oz. tomato paste

Optional

- Vegan Parmesan
- Fresh basil

Directions

1. Soak the cashews in water to hasten the cooking process.
2. Add all the ingredients (except the cashews) to the slow cooker. Simmer on low heat with a lid on for six hours.
3. Put the cashews that have been soaking in an immersion blender.
4. Top with chosen toppings and serve warm.

Nutrition Info:

- KCal 284, Fat 9 g, Carbs 42 g, Protein 10 g

54. Spicy Indian Beef Roast

- Serves: 8
- Cook Time: 10 hr.

Ingredients

- 2 red onions, diced
- 2 tablespoons freshly squeezed lemon juice
- 4 cloves of garlic, minced
- 1 ½-inch ginger, minced
- 25 curry leaves
- 1 serrano pepper, minced
- 1 tbsp. meat masala
- 2 tbsp. coconut oil
- 1 tsp. black mustard seed
- 2 ½ pounds grass-fed beef roast

Directions:

1. Everything should be placed inside the Crock-Pot.
2. Give it a good stir.
3. Place the lid firmly in place and cook on high for 6 hours or on low for 10 hours.

Nutrition Info:

- KCal: 222; Carbs: 1.1g; Protein: 31.3g; Fat:10.4 g

55. *Italian Meatball Soup*

- Serves 8

Ingredients

- 1 (10-oz.) bag frozen soup vegetables
- Some fresh oregano (optional)
- 2 (14½-oz.) cans Italian-style tomatoes, diced, undrained
- 2 (12-oz.) bags Italian-style turkey meatballs, thawed and cooked
- 1 (15-oz.) can black beans, rinsed, drained
- 1 (14-oz.) can seasoned chicken broth with roasted garlic

Directions

1. In a bowl, combine all ingredients except the oregano.
2. Place all the ingredients in a slow cooker set to LOW and simmer for 6 to 7 hours.
3. You may also cook it for three to three and a half hours on HIGH if you're in a hurry.
4. Transfer to a bowl and add oregano, if desired.
5. Get ready and enjoy.

Nutrition Info:

- KCal 287, Fat 13 g, Carbs 30 g, Protein 16 g

56. *Split Pea Soup*

- Serves 4

Ingredients

- 1 pound split peas, rinsed and dried
- 6 C. vegetable broth

- 1 onion, diced
- 1 bay leaf
- 1 tsp. thyme
- Salt and pepper (to taste)
- 1 tsp. cumin
- 1 tsp. sage
- 2 carrots, peeled and chopped
- 2 chopped celery stalks and 3 minced garlic cloves

Directions

1. After adding everything, turn the crock pot down to low. Cover and slowly heat for at least 4 hours.
2. Serve straight away or use an immersion blender to puree until smooth.

Nutrition Info:

- KCal 272, Fat 1 g, Carbs 75 g, Protein 25 g

57. French Canadian Pea Soup

- Serves 8-10

Ingredients

- 2 C. yellow peas
- 1 ham hock or 6 oz. salted pork belly
- 1 onion, finely diced
- ½ tsp. dried savory (optional)
- Salt and black pepper, to taste
- 6 C. water

Directions

1. Give the peas an overnight soak in water. If necessary, rinse and sort the peas. Empty.
2. To the slow cooker, add the peas, onion, ham hock or salted pork belly, and savory, if using.

3. Simmer on LOW for 8 to 10 hours with a lid on.

4. Remove the ham hock or salt pork. After the pork has cooled for a few minutes, remove any leftover meat off the bone or salted meat.

5. Re-add the meat to the slow cooker, stir it around to ensure uniform cooking, and then set the timer for a further 10 to 15 minutes.

6. If needed, add more salt and pepper to taste.

7. Toast the bread and serve it hot.

Nutrition Info:

- KCal 191, Fat 6 g, Carbs 24 g, Protein 10 g

58. Cajun Sausage and White Bean Soup

- Serves 6

Ingredients

- 1 tablespoon red wine vinegar
- Add pepper and salt.
- Low-sodium chicken broth (8 C.)
- 2 celery stalks, chopped
- 4 fresh thyme sprigs
- 8 C. collard greens, leaves only, cut to 1-inch pieces
- 1 pound dried Great Northern beans
- ½ pound Cajun andouille sausage, sliced
- 1 large onion, diced

Directions

1. Set aside the final three ingredients.

2. In a slow cooker, add cooked beans, sausage, onion, celery, thyme, and chicken broth.

3. Cook, covered, on LOW for 7–8 hours or, on HIGH for 4–5 hours. The best beans are tender ones.

4. Remove the thyme stalks and stir in the collard greens. Cover and simmer for a further 15 minutes to thoroughly cook the greens.
5. Add the vinegar, pepper, and salt together.

Nutrition Info:

- KCal 393, Fat 8 g, Carbs 51 g, Protein 30 g

59.   *Chipotle Chicken Soup*

- Serves 4

Ingredients

- 1 tsp. black pepper
- 1 tsp. cumin
- 1 tsp. salt
- 1 C. onion, sliced
- ¼ C. chipotle chili in adobo sauce, diced
- 4 C. chicken stock
- ½ tsp. coriander
- 1 C. poblano pepper, sliced
- 1 avocado, sliced
- 1 cup shredded Monterey Jack cheese and ½ cup fresh cilantro
- 1 pound boneless chicken pieces
- 1 tbsp. olive oil

Directions

1. Finely chop the chicken into small pieces.
2. Drizzle the chicken with olive oil after seasoning it with salt, pepper, cumin, and coriander.
3. In a slow cooker, combine the chicken, poblano, onion, chipotle, and adobo sauce; simmer on low for eight hours.
4. Add the chicken stock, place a lid on it, and let it simmer on high for four hours, making sure to check on the chicken every now and then.

5. A flavorful garnish for the soup consists of chopped cilantro, Monterey Jack cheese, and avocado slices.

Nutrition Info:

- KCal 363, Fat 20.9 g, Carbs 10.5 g, Protein 33.7 g

DESSERT RECIPES

60. Nutty Caramel Apples

- Servings: 6
- Cook Time: 4 Hrs.

Ingredients:

- 6 gala apples, cut in half and deseeded
- 8 oz caramel, package
- 5 tbsp water
- 3 tbsp walnuts, crushed

Directions:

1. Combine the apples, water, caramel, and walnuts in a Crock Pot insert.
2. Close the cooker's cover and select the Low Cook Time option of three hours.
3. Once chilled, serve.

Nutrition Info:

- KCal: 307, Total Fat: 12g, Fiber: 5g, Total Carbs: 47.17g, Protein: 4g

61. Orange Bowls

- Cook: 3 hours
- Servings: 2

Ingredients:

- ½ pound oranges, peeled and cut into segments
- 1 cup heavy cream
- ½ tablespoon almonds, chopped
- 1 tablespoon chia seeds
- 1 tablespoon sugar

Directions:

1. Combine the oranges, cream, and the rest of the ingredients in your slow cooker. Give it a good shake, cover it, and simmer for three hours on the lowest heat.
2. To serve, divide the mixture among serving dishes.

Nutrition:

- Kcal 170, fat 0, fiber 2, carbs 7, protein 4

62. *Apple Compote*

- Cook: 1 hour
- Servings: 2

Ingredients:

- Apples weighing one pound each, cored and segmented into wedges
- 1/2 a cup of water
- 1 teaspoon equivalent of sugar
- 1 milliliter of pure vanilla essence
- 1/2 milliliter of almond extract

Directions:

1. Add the apples, water, and remaining ingredients to your slow cooker. Give everything a good stir, put a lid on, and cook for an hour on High.
2. Serve the mixture in bowls and at room temperature.

Nutrition:

- Kcal 203, fat 0, fiber 1, carbs 5, protein 4

63.   *Vanilla Grapes Mix*

- Cook: 2 hours
- Servings: 2

Ingredients:

- 1 cup grapes, halved
- 1/2 milliliter of pure vanilla essence
- 1 cup of oranges, which have been peeled and segmented.
- ¼ cup water
- 1 and ½ tablespoons sugar
- 1 teaspoon lemon juice

Directions:

1. To prepare the grapes, fill a slow cooker with the oranges, water, and remaining ingredients. Mix everything well, put a lid on, and cook on Low for two hours.
2. To serve, divide the mixture among serving dishes.

Nutrition:

- Kcal 100, fat 3, fiber 6, carbs 8, protein 3

64.   *Quinoa Pudding*

- Cook: 2 hours
- Servings: 2

Ingredients:

- 1 cup quinoa
- 2 cups almond milk

- ½ cup sugar
- ½ tablespoon walnuts, chopped
- ½ tablespoon almonds, chopped

Directions:

1. Combine the quinoa, milk, and other ingredients in your slow cooker. Give everything a good stir, put a lid on, and simmer for two hours on High.
2. Serve the pudding after dividing it into parts.

Nutrition:

- Kcal 213, fat 4, fiber 6, carbs 10, protein 4

65. *Lemony Orange Marmalade*

- Servings: 8
- Cook Time: 3 Hrs.

Ingredients:

- Juice of 2 lemons
- 3 lbs. sugar
- 1 lb. oranges, stripped and cut into segments
- 1-pint water

Directions:

1. Add oranges to the Crock Pot insert along with sugar, water, and lemon juice.
2. Place a lid on the slow cooker and program it to cook on High for three hours.
3. Serve cold for optimal flavor.

Nutrition Info:

- KCal: 100, Fiber: 4g, Total Carbs: 12g, Protein: 4g

66. *Mandarin Cream*

- Servings: 2
- Cook Time: 2 Hr.

Ingredients:

- 1 tbsp. ginger, grated
- 3 tbsp. sugar
- 3 mandarins, stripped and diced
- 2 tbsp. agave nectar
- ½ C. coconut cream

Directions:

1. Stir together the ginger, sugar, mandarins, and remaining ingredients in the crock pot. Simmer for two hours on High with a cover on.
2. After smoothing the cream with an immersion blender, store it in the refrigerator and serve it in individual servings.

Nutrition Info:

- KCal100, fat 4, fiber 5, carbs 6, protein 7

67. *Mascarpone With Strawberry Jelly*

- Servings:6
- Cook Time: 1 Hr.

Ingredients:

- 2 C. strawberries, diced
- 1 tbsp. gelatin
- 3 tbsp. sugar
- ¼ C. of water
- 1 C. mascarpone

Directions:

1. Strawberries and sugar should be combined, then blended until smooth.
2. Place it inside the Crock Pot and simmer for one hour on High.
3. In the interim, combine water and gelatin.
4. Beat the mascarpone thoroughly.
5. After cooking, allow the strawberry mixture to cool somewhat before adding the gelatin. Mix it carefully.
6. After filling the ramekins with the strawberry mixture, chill for two hours.
7. Then top the jelly with whisked mascarpone.

Nutrition Info:

- 125 kCal, 9g protein, 11g Carbs, 5.5g fat

68. Easy Monkey Rolls

- Servings:8
- Cook Time: 3 Hr.

Ingredients:

- 1 tbsp. liquid honey
- 1 tbsp. sugar
- 2 eggs, beaten
- 1-pound cinnamon rolls, dough
- 2 tbsp. butter, melted

Directions:

1. Cut the cinnamon roll dough into eight equal parts.
2. Arrange the rolls in a Crock Pot that has been lined with parchment paper.
3. Beat the butter and sugar together until a ball is formed. Combine the ingredients by whisking them together.
4. Evenly spread out the dough for the cinnamon rolls, then cover it with the egg mixture.
5. Cook, covered, over high heat for three hours.

Nutrition Info:

- 266 kCal, 4.9g protein, 32.6g Carbs, 13.3g fat,

69. Braised Pears

- Servings:6
- Cook Time: 2.5 Hr.

Ingredients:

- 6 pears
- 2 C. wine
- 1 tbsp. sugar
- 1 cinnamon stick

Directions:

1. Place the peeled halves inside the slow cooker.
2. Replace the lid and stir in the remaining ingredients.
3. Cook the pears on High for about 2.5 hours.
4. Serve the hot wine mixture alongside the pears.

Nutrition Info:

- 210 kCal, 1.1g protein, 38g Carbs, 1.1g fat

70. Cherry and Rhubarb Mix

- Cook: 2 hours

- Servings: 2

Ingredients:

- 2 cups rhubarb, sliced
- ½ cup cherries, pitted
- 1 tablespoon butter, melted
- ¼ cup coconut cream
- ½ cup sugar

Directions:

1. In the slow cooker with the cherries and the rest of the ingredients, prepare the rhubarb. Shake everything well, cover, and cook for two hours on High.
2. Pour the mixture into individual bowls and serve chilled.

Nutrition:

- Kcal 200, fat 2, fiber 3, carbs 6, protein 1

71. *Delightful Cardamom Apples*

- Cook: 2 hours
- Servings: 2

Ingredients:

- 1-pound apples, cored and cut into wedges
- ½ cup almond milk
- ¼ teaspoon cardamom, ground
- 2 tablespoons brown sugar

Directions:

1. To prepare the apples, fill your slow cooker with the cardamom and remaining ingredients. Shake well, cover, and simmer on High for two hours.
2. Pour the mixture into individual bowls and serve chilled.

Nutrition:

- Kcal 280, fat 2, fiber 1, carbs 10, protein 6

72. Peaches and Wine Sauce

- Cook: 2 hours
- Servings: 2

Ingredients:

- 3 tablespoons of granulated or brown sugar
- Peaches weighing one pound each, cored and cut into wedges
- ½ cup of crimson wine
- ½ milliliter of pure vanilla essence
- 1 grated milligram of lemon zest in a serving

Directions:

1. In your slow cooker, combine the peaches, sugar, and remaining ingredients. Stir well, cover, and simmer on High for two hours.
2. Divide the mixture among dishes for serving.

Nutrition:

- Kcal 200, fat 4, fiber 6, carbs 9, protein 4

73. Peach Cream

- Cook: 3 hours
- Servings: 2

Ingredients:

- ¼ teaspoon cinnamon powder
- 1 cup peaches, pitted and chopped
- ¼ cup heavy cream

- Cooking spray
- 1 tablespoon maple syrup
- ½ teaspoons vanilla extract
- 2 tablespoons sugar

Directions:

1. Process the peaches, cinnamon, and all other ingredients (except the nonstick cooking spray) in a food processor or blender until smooth.
2. Cooking spray should be used inside the slow cooker before adding the cream mixture, covering, and cooking on Low for three hours.
3. Transfer the cream into dishes and serve it room temperature.

Nutrition:

- Kcal 200, fat 3, fiber 4, carbs 10, protein 9

74. *Pomegranate and Mango Bowls*

- Cook: 3 hours
- Servings: 2

Ingredients:

- Pomegranate seeds, enough to fill 2 cups
- 1 ounce of mango, peeled and cut into little pieces
- ½ cup of full-fat heavy cream
- 1 tablespoon of juice from a lemon
- ½ milliliter of pure vanilla essence
- 2 teaspoons of refined white sugar

Directions:

1. In your slow cooker, combine the mango, pomegranate seeds, and remaining ingredients. Stir well, cover, and simmer on the lowest setting for three hours.
2. The combination should be served room temperature and in bowls.

Nutrition:

- Kcal 162, fat 4, fiber 5, carbs 20, protein 6

75. *Easy Blueberries Jam*

- Cook: 4 hours
- Servings: 2

Ingredients:

- 2 measures (cups) of blueberries
- ½ cup water
- ¼ pound sugar
- Zest of 1 lime

Directions:

1. Fill your slow cooker with the berries, water, and remaining ingredients. Shake well, cover, and simmer on High for 4 hours.
2. Once the mixture is separated, serve it chilled in jars.

Nutrition:

- Kcal 250, fat 3, fiber 2, carbs 6, protein 1

76. *Stuffed Peaches*

- Servings:4
- Cook Time: 20 Min.

Ingredients:

- 4 peaches, halved, pitted
- 4 pecans
- 1 tbsp. maple syrup
- 2 oz goat cheese, crumbled

Directions:

1. Place a pecan within each half of a peach and drizzle with maple syrup.
2. Spreading the goat cheese on top of the fruit in the Crock Pot is the next step.
3. Close the top and cook the peaches on high heat for 20 minutes.

Nutrition Info:

- 234 kCal, 7.2g protein, 19.7g Carbs, 15.5g fat

77. Cinnamon Rice Milk Cocktail

- Servings:6
- Cook Time: 1.5 Hr.

Ingredients:

- 1 C. long-grain rice
- ½ C. agave syrup
- 3 C. of water
- 1 tsp. crushed cinnamon
- 1 banana, diced

Directions:

1. You should put the rice in the processor.
2. Pour the mixture into a blender and thin with water.
3. The liquid should then be strained and added to the slow cooker.
4. Add ground cinnamon and agave nectar and blend. On High, the liquid needs to cook for 1.5 hours.
5. Pouring the hot liquid into the food processor or blender is the next step.
6. Add a banana and blend until very smooth.

Nutrition Info:

- 215 kCal, 2.4g protein, 51.5g Carbs, 0.3g fat

78. *Apricot Spoon Cake*

- Servings:10
- Cook Time: 2.5 Hr.

Ingredients:

- 2 C. cake mix
- 1 C. milk
- 1 C. apricots, canned, pitted, diced, with juice
- 2 eggs, beaten
- 1 tbsp. sunflower oil

Directions:

1. Combine cake mix, egg, and milk.
2. Next add the sunflower oil and process the blend until it's smooth.
3. Next, line the Crock Pot with baking paper.
4. After adding the cake mix batter to the slow cooker, lightly push it down and cover.
5. On High, bake the cake for 2.5 hours.
6. After that, slide the cooked cake onto the platter and drizzle with apricot jam and cherries.
7. Allow the cake to warm up before slicing it into portions.

Nutrition Info:

- 268 kCal, 4.5g protein, 43.8g Carbs, 8.6g fat

79. *Baked Goat Cheese Balls*

- Servings:6
- Cook Time: 1 Hr.

Ingredients:

- 1 tsp. butter
- 1 tbsp. breadcrumbs

- 8 oz goat cheese
- 4 tbsp. sesame seeds
- 1 tsp. of sugar powder

Directions:

1. Combine breadcrumbs, sugar powder, and goat cheese.
2. Roll into medium-sized balls and roll in sesame seeds.
3. Pour the melted butter into the Crock Pot.
4. After adding the balls to the slow cooker, cover it with a single layer.
5. On high heat, prepare the sweet for one hour.

Nutrition Info:

- 217 kCal, 12.8g protein, 3.5g Carbs, 17.1g fat

80. *Mango Cream Dessert*

- Servings: 4
- Cook Time: 1 Hr.

Ingredients:

- 1 mango, sliced
- 14 oz. coconut cream

Directions:

1. Mango and cream should be added to the Crock Pot insert.
2. Secure the cooker's lid and set the temperature to High, with a cooking duration of 1 hour.
3. Assist.

Nutrition Info:

- KCal: 150, Fiber: 2g, Total Carbs: 6g, Protein: 1g

CONCLUSION

We turn the last page of this Crock Pot Cookbook to finish our trip through the art of slow cooking. The main idea behind this book is simple: you don't have to spend a lot of time in the kitchen to make delicious meals with basic items. This article talks about how a crock pot can make cooking food for yourself and your family easier and better. The slow cooker has shown that it is more than just an appliance; it makes it easier to make delicious meals that feed people and inspire their imagination in the kitchen. It can be used to make many different kinds of food, from simple veggie sides to fancy sweets.

We started with the basics: learning how to use your crock pot properly and understanding how to set it up. To make sure that every dish had the right texture and taste complexity, it was important to master time and temperature. We talked about how important it is to carefully choose the ingredients, like the types of meat and veggies and the liquid bases that make broths and sauces taste great. The goal of these technical tips was to help you get the best position and give you trust in your ability to easily make any meal.

After looking at the recipes, it was clear that there are a lot of different foods that can be made to suit different tastes and nutritional needs. The crock pot can make a wide range of foods, from traditional comfort foods like beef stew and chicken and dumplings to healthier choices like vegetable lentil soup and slow-cooked quinoa bowls. This means it can fit a wide range of lifestyles. You now know how to make slow cooking more interesting by adding different flavors, trying out different spices, and having fresh ingredients. This book showed that even on the busiest weeknights, you can make delicious dinners with just a little planning and drive.

This guide focuses on a bigger idea that goes beyond the recipes and can be used in situations other than cooking. Instead of just a way to cook food, slow cooking is a way of thinking about food. Realizing that cooking takes a long time and not rushing or making things too complicated are part of it. It has to do with letting tastes develop. This way of cooking slows things down so we can enjoy the experience more in a world that moves too quickly. The crock pot shows how convenience and quality can live together peacefully. It lets us feed our family and ourselves without giving up taste, imagination, or time.

This book gives you the skills to turn everyday things into fancy foods that look like they take a lot of work to make. Each chapter, suggestion, and recipe has been carefully written to show that the crock pot is useful for more than just making easy meals or taking shortcuts. It is a way to improve taste, make cooking more enjoyable, and make your life easier without lowering the quality of what you make. No matter if you're cooking for yourself or for a family meeting, there are many foods that can make you feel good and save you time.

If this guide has taught you anything, I hope it's that cooking is important even if it's hard or takes a lot of time. With the new knowledge and tools you've gained, you can now approach making meals in a different way, one that values simplicity without losing taste or fun. From what we've seen, the crock pot is a hidden hero of the kitchen. It works quietly while you go about your day, making sure that the food will be as relaxing as the process of making it.

This book should serve as a reminder to you as you continue to discover the possibilities of your slow cooker: all it takes is a little preparation, a little imagination, and the perfect recipe to create delicious meals. You can now make meals that taste as though they took hours to prepare, and they also give you the flexibility to savor the moments in between.

Made in the USA
Columbia, SC
07 December 2024

48695988R00057